DOUBLE
MELANCHOLY

Art, Beauty, and the

DOUBLE

Making of a

MELANCHOLY

Brown Queer Man

C.E. GATCHALIAN

ARSENAL PULP PRESS
VANCOUVER

DOUBLE MELANCHOLY
Copyright © 2019 by C.E. Gatchalian

ARSENAL PULP PRESS
Suite 202 – 211 East Georgia St.
Vancouver, BC V6A 1Z6
Canada
arsenalpulp.com

The publisher gratefully acknowledges the support of the Canada Council for the Arts and the British Columbia Arts Council for its publishing program, and the Government of Canada, and the Government of British Columbia (through the Book Publishing Tax Credit Program), for its publishing activities.

Arsenal Pulp Press acknowledges the xʷməθkʷə̓y̓əm (Musqueam), Sḵwx̱wú7mesh (Squamish), and səlilwətaʔɬ (Tsleil-Waututh) Nations, speakers of Hul'q'umi'num'/Halq'eméylem/hən̓q̓əmin̓əm̓ and custodians of the traditional, ancestral, and unceded territories where our office is located. We pay respect to their histories, traditions, and continuous living cultures and commit to accountability, respectful relations, and friendship.

"Retreat: A Streetcar Named Desire" was previously published, in slightly different form, in *Plenitude* magazine (December 2017). "Divine: Maria Callas" was previously published, in substantially different form, in *Ricepaper* magazine and in the anthologies *Best Canadian Essays 2011* (Tightrope Books) and *AlliterAsian: Twenty Years of Ricepaper Magazine* (Arsenal Pulp Press, 2015).

Song lyrics for "I'm Not Sorry" by Kimmortal used by permission of the artist.

Cover and text design by Oliver McPartlin
Edited by Shirarose Wilensky
Proofread by Alison Strobel

Printed and bound in Canada

Library and Archives Canada Cataloguing in Publication:
Gatchalian, C. E., 1974–, author
    Double melancholy : art, beauty, and the making of a brown queer man / C.E. Gatchalian.
Issued in print and electronic formats.
ISBN 978-1-55152-753-6 (softcover).—ISBN 978-1-55152-754-3 (HTML)
    1. Art and society. 2. Art—Philosophy. 3. Literature and society.
4. Gatchalian, C. E., 1974–. I. Title.
N72.S6G38 2019   701'.03   C2018-906216-9
                                         C2018-906217-7

To the unceded, unsurrendered, ancestral territories of the Musqueam, Squamish and Tsleil-Waututh nations, a.k.a. Vancouver. The lands that I've lived on my whole life, that inform how I write, that I love.

"The only books that influence us are those for which we are ready, and which have gone a little further down our particular path than we have yet got ourselves."
—E.M. Forster, *Two Cheers for Democracy*

CONTENTS

ACKNOWLEDGMENTS

First and foremost, the wonderful, smart, supportive folks at Arsenal Pulp Press, for believing in and shepherding *Double Melancholy*: Brian Lam, Shirarose Wilensky, Oliver McPartlin, Cynara Geissler, and Susan Safyan.

I'd like to thank the Canada Council for the Arts, the British Columbia Arts Council, and the Fund for the Arts on the North Shore for financially supporting the writing of this book.

I'd like to thank Todd Wong and Ann-Marie Metten for making possible my residency at Kogawa House, where more than half of this book was written. And a special, separate thanks to Todd for his generous friendship the last few years, which has played a large part in my being able to live and work as an artist in my beloved, increasingly unaffordable hometown.

Thanks to my fellow scribe Lucia Frangione and her partner, Scott Johnson, for making their beautiful Joy Tide Suite on Bowen Island available for me to complete the writing of this book.

Thanks to Dalbir Singh and Martin Kinch for their in-depth reading of the manuscript, as well as Valerie Sing Turner for her thoughtful, eloquent feedback.

And, finally, a big thank you to my personal support system the last few years: Chris, Casey, Katie, and, as always, my mother. In these few years I've experienced what have been both my toughest struggles and my greatest triumphs as an artist. You helped me through them.

PRELUDE TO A FUGUE

"*Vissi d'arte.*"

Like Tosca, I live for art.

Many people—especially those who belong to the creative class—possess a pantheon of books, films, and other cultural artifacts that is as much a reflection of their personal obsessions as it is a gauge of their aesthetic tastes.

For queer men, it is possible to speak of a common pantheon, because our shared experiences of sex and love—the grist for most art, both high and low—bind us to a common lovelorn mentality. The objects of our desire are too often unattainable, so our point of view is always tinged with unrequited love, making the pantheon an opportunistic ladder to wish-fulfillment. When the real world is hostile, uncomprehending, or indifferent, books, movies, and TV shows nourish, answer the call, fill the void.

If the above sounds hackneyed, it's because I make no attempt in this book to be original. I embrace and perpetuate stereotypes—they ward off wholesale historical erasure. For as a brown queer man, erasure is what I struggle against—have always struggled against—even though I came late to being able to name it. Stereotypes are, of course, horrible, but not quite as horrible as invisibility.

For me, the stereotypes are actually fairly accurate: domineering mother, absent father. I preferred art and literature to sports and video games as a child, found an outlet in academics while other boys found it in flogging the log, was a late bloomer sexually, have been feverishly promiscuous, suffer from anxiety and obsessive compulsive disorder. And I love Maria Callas and Billie Holiday.

But these facts, for me, are not objects of shame but rather the necessary constituents of my intellectual and artistic matrix. I embrace them, same as what I consider to be, in my more self-delighting moments, my cultural lineage: Walter Pater, John Addington Symonds, Oscar Wilde, Henry James, Thomas Mann, E.M. Forster, Marcel Proust, Tennessee Williams, Edward Albee. The homosexual as culture-maker, antennae to the heavens, freed from the burdens of marriage and family to focus on the unnecessary and beautiful. The homosexual as modern-day incarnation of the shaman, possessor of special knowledge, calendar-keeper of the world.

This book is about striving, the striving caused by double melancholy: the melancholy of being queer, the melancholy of being brown. (And the melancholy of seeking heavenly transcendence on earth, and earthly justice in heaven.) And with double melancholy comes the doubling of the intensity of this striving for success, for perfection, for orgasm, for the divine.

Melancholy. As Didier Eribon posits in *Insult and the Making of the Gay Self*, this is where it all starts and, in fact, ends—the lifelong process of mourning that each homosexual goes through, and through which we construct our individual identities. It is mourning for the loss of heterosexual privilege: of easy and automatic familial and social approval, of universally sanctioned unions and family units, of seeing one's reflections in the dominant myths of romantic culture. It is to combat this melancholy that we build, sculpt, etch, paint, compose, write—at a level, as I've heard even homophobes concede, higher, on average, than our heterosexual fellow travellers. Although straights may indeed face their own romantic and family quandaries, these cannot equate to the systemic barriers homosexuals everywhere confront. These are barriers against the expression of our most powerful, intimate feelings, which beget melancholy and have, in turn, begotten some of the world's greatest art. Every sketch, every splash of colour, every appoggiatura, every rigorously wrought iamb is a stay we erect against the hostile flood of the main current.

But where does melancholy reside in this age of greater acceptance (at least in the West), when equal marriage, anti-discrimination, and anti-bullying are becoming the laws of the land? Is speaking of melancholy as a creative catalyst mere nostalgia, a contrivance to keep homosexuals a romantically oppressed minority?

Melancholy can happen when we spot a handsome man on the street and acknowledge, after daydreaming about all we'd like to do with him, that he is unattainable because in all likelihood he bats for the other team. To say the least, this is maudlin compared to the horrors queers face in places like Uganda; still, the cumulative effect is that of perpetual rejection. Camille Paglia may be correct, in part, when in *Vamps & Tramps* she calls homosexuality "inherently tragic," since "it posits as glamorous perfection precisely what most loathes it and cancels it out." She is certainly correct when she adds that "from this agonizing and irresolvable contradiction came some of our greatest art, such as that of Donatello, Botticelli, and Michelangelo."

And there is the added melancholy of being a brown person in a predominantly white space. For melancholy also happens when we spot a handsome Caucasian guy in the club and know that it's quite likely we have no chance whatsoever with him. "I'm not racist," we imagine him saying. "I have lots of non-white friends. But sexually, I'm only into white dudes." Of course, one can argue that the only way to find out for sure is to ask him outright, but the brain doesn't care whether the rejection is imagined or real. Trauma has already occurred; the damage is done.

The melancholy of being brown in a white society, I've realized, is even profounder than that of queerness. For if whiteness defines everything, including how we think and speak of queerness, how can the brown queer man not feel like an exile?

But, as both Nietzsche and Heidegger taught us, conflict is creative. Out of disappointment and despair spring fresco, rondo, and rhyme—a mantra I like to return to whenever I experience adversity, whether a petty slight to my ego or an account of anti-queer stonings in Iran.

Melancholy. Whether a result of my shunning the world because it was hostile and intolerant or the world's shunning me because I was sullen and contrary—melancholy became my default internal state. But it wasn't one I fell into with resistance or resentment; somehow, even as a youngster, I simply accepted it as fact that the only truly safe space for me would be inside my own mind, my own abstruse, esoteric interior world. It was one, indeed, refined in the extreme, permitting only the densest texts, the most rarefied music. The more difficult the art, the deeper my retreat into the safety and (at least in my own self-justifying imagination) infinite superiority of melancholy.

There was perhaps the possibility of melancholy's end—or, at least, alleviation—with adulthood, active sexuality, and full membership in the queer community. But that optimism was crushed by that community's white supremacy. Melancholy, I came to realize, would be chronic.

So, no, melancholy is no mere romantic contrivance—as long as I'm brown and queer, it is both the wound that won't close and the soul-force that motors me skyward.

This book is a performance—a performance of decolonization. (Or at least an attempt at one—my newfound anti-colonialism must favour statements more modest in scope.) It acknowledges both how these (mostly white, largely Eurocentric) artworks brought me personal edification, and how, simultaneously, they invisibilized my political and social identities. The position I describe is one of radical synthesis: I wish to hold ostensibly incompatible points of view at the same time. So I allow, in this book, for a multiplicity of voices: there is the voice I am deploying now—the voice proper of the book—and the two voices that weave a fugue with it, respectively grounding and undermining it. There's the voice of my personal journals (the first entry dating from age nine), contextualizing the voice proper's critical abstractions with sometimes painfully intimate autobiographical details (I've always been an obsessive diary-keeper, probably because, at bottom, I need proof that *I exist*). And there's the voice in parentheses, the voice of my philosophical radicalism—recalcitrant against erasure and obsessively pure in its ideology. On the personal level, this vocal fragmentation embraces vulnerability; on the political, it resists the imperial implications of the singular voice.

In the spirit of decolonization, the ethnic identifier I now choose for myself is "Filipinx," rather than the more common "Filipino." Tagalog—the language of my ancestors, whose standardized form, Filipino, is the official native language of the Philippines—is essentially non-gendered, but three centuries of Spanish colonization brought gender to the proceedings, as reflected in the suffixes of certain words ("o" denoting male and "a" denoting female). "Filipinx" performs a much-needed linguistic disruption to this colonization by defying the Eurocentric gender binary and refusing to privilege masculinity.

———————

Most of the art I love is the product of processes that have diminished my existence as a brown queer man. I want to acknowledge this grim reality while reiterating my love for the art that made me.

(It's not possible.

Also, have you noticed the patrician tone of the narrator's writing? He's Filipinx: their written English is known to be quaintly formal—probably a gesture of deference to their American colonizers, whose own English was inherited, making Filipinx English doubly bastardized. As a Filipinx Canadian, you might say his English is thrice *removed.)*

Then why this emphasis on identity? Art has afforded me spiritual edification; haven't I thereby, in effect, reached the ultimate realm? Isn't concern with the "lower" strata of worldly inequities therefore moot?

To bypass the "lower" realm is to bypass the experience of my communities: queer folks, racialized folks, queer racialized folks. It is also to bypass my place and worth in the world, as a person whose history is as innately valuable as a heteronormative white man's.

I fully subscribe to the idea that great art (like great sex, like non-divisive, non-coercive forms of religion and spirituality) is a means to the release and letting-go of self. But, to paraphrase the most grounded and socially engaged Buddhist teachers, one must *have* a self before one can let go of it.

And why this reliance on artworks as a syllabus for living? I was alienated enough as a brown child; being queer intensified this alienation tenfold. There was no one in my inner sanctum I felt I could talk to about my feelings and, consequently, no one whose way of moving in the world I could use as a template. Inevitably, more often than not, I had to look outside of home and school for these templates, and although this enriched my imagination, it did nothing for my street savvy. This may explain, at least partly, many of the poor choices I've made in my romantic life.

This book is about *my* striving, not anyone else's—though many queer men, especially queer men of colour, will probably, I venture to guess, see much of their own trajectories in mine. I'm quite certain there will be straight, trans, and lesbian fellow travellers as well. Indeed, the foremost figure behind the book is a lesbian: Susan Sontag hovers under these essays like an elemental force, heavy and humourless but at the same time Daedalus-like, a wing-maker of sorts to her addled and hungry queer acolytes. But she makes clear, in her legendary book *Against Interpretation*, that we are, and always will be, failures, even as she gives us wings: "As the corrupt Alcibiades followed Socrates, unable and unwilling to change his own life, but moved, enriched and full of love, so the sensitive modern reader pays his respect to a level of spiritual reality which is not and could not be his own."

So what matters, again, is the striving, the perpetual climb up the unclimbable, the struggle to—in Samuel Beckett's words—"fail better." Thus we become *bons vivants*, Sontagian "besotted aesthetes": whether dilettante or maestro, we—to paraphrase what Roland Barthes said of the strident, starry-eyed Sontag—row and row and row.

Fail better. This, in part, is what accounts for my besottedness: the failed staircase to the truth is aglitter with Arnoldian delights (as in Matthew Arnold, the Victorian poet and social theorist branded by many as an elitist for defining culture as "the best of what has been thought and said")—models of the striving and serious, some of whom play prominent roles in this book, such as E.M. Forster, Tennessee Williams, Thomas Mann, and Maria Callas. Two of the book's essays are on subjects—*Anne of Green Gables*, the British miniseries *Queer as Folk*, —that Arnoldian purists will suggest more properly belong to the popular realm. I accept this protest with defiance and pride, as evidence of my newfound resistance to wholesale colonization. For to embrace aspects of pop culture is a flip-off to cultural conservatives who believe Western high art to be the only culture—besides Christianity—worth embracing.

(It's safe to assume that, in reality, his embrace of pop culture is inspired by early Sontag, who shook the cultural scene in the sixties with her eloquent apologias, only to turn her back on pop culture later in life in favour of Great Literature. Also, embracing pop culture by itself is not anti-colonial, given how pop culture—much more than high art—teems with the biases and prejudices of mainstream society.

More generally, we must note the compulsiveness of the narrator's habitual turning to art—the shameless revelling and name-dropping.

He fetishizes this space so graciously permitted him—this library, this cinematheque, this staircase.

Is this book itself a fetish object for similarly besotted, politically anemic aesthetes?)

My name is Christopher Edwin Gatchalian. I'm a writer based in Vancouver, British Columbia, Canada. I was named after Christopher Plummer, whom my mother developed a crush on after seeing *The Sound of Music*. My pen name—C.E. Gatchalian—I modelled after one of my literary heroes: T.S. Eliot.

This book is about how I, as a brown queer man, made the best out of the narrow space allowed me, and, in the process, made myself both invisible and fiercely alive.

1 | *RUPTURE:* ANNE OF GREEN GABLES

Even as a young child, I knew I was odd. But that doesn't necessarily mean I always felt at odds with the world.

In the beginning, before the rupture, was pure consciousness. I was one with the world; my rhythms were its rhythms. Even after the inevitable ego boundaries had formed and I'd realized that my will was not necessarily the will of the universe, I still felt—until the age of ten—enough concord with the world to not feel particularly estranged by it.

On the contrary—I thought the world my oyster. I was an only child; my father left us when I was three. Consequently, there was no one with whom I had to compete for my mother's attention (at least not early on; later, her boyfriends would wreak havoc on our mystical union). As well, I was reading fluently by age three and by age four had taught myself to play piano by ear. I was identified as "gifted" and treated duly by the adults around me. I was "well behaved" and "conscientious," according to my grade two report card. Only child, teacher's pet. As a child, I had some privilege.

June 5, 1983

[my earliest surviving journal entry]

Upon blowing out my birthday candles on this, the night of my ninth birthday, I made the following wishes (I know we're only supposed to make one, but I made three, because I can):

1. That I get straight As in school this year (yes, even math, and PE doesn't count—only ignoramuses get As in PE)

2. That I get the highest mark in the province on my grade four piano exam

3. That we win the dream house at this year's PNE [Pacific National Exhibition, Vancouver's annual summer trashy, petit bourgeois fun fair]

I visualized all three of these things happening just before I blew my candles out, because everything I set my heart on, I get. Always. I am a good person and I work hard and I deserve it.

I don't remember there being a birthday party for me that year. In fact, I think I was thrown only two birthday parties my entire childhood—not because my mother was anti-social or stingy, but because of my own, seemingly innate, aversion to anything that smacked of society (except school—I welcomed it as society's proxy, as the thing to struggle against and transcend). Parties seemed to *celebrate* society—and why would anyone want to do something as insipid as that?

So as a child, my political leanings were anti-collectivist; I subscribed to a philosophy of meritocratic, heroic individualism. I attribute this early political conservatism to my mother, who remains the fiercest embodiment I know of unadulterated self-reliance. When she separated from my father—with whom she immigrated to Canada from the Philippines three years before I was born—she was ostracized by her Filipinx friends, whose ethics dictated they render my parents immoral. And although the dictum was officially about both of them, it was my mother who bore the brunt of it; in Filipinx culture, as in many others, the wife is expected to endure all of the husband's transgressions.

Being branded a "bad woman" turned my mother off community, so she disentangled herself from the mob and focused single-mindedly on motherhood. This worked out well for me, but there were other benefits as well: when my mother severed ties with her community, she also severed ties with that community's hegemon: the Church. So I was spared the autocratic indignities forced upon most Filipinx children: attending Mass, serving at Mass, Sunday school, Catholic school. I was baptized but never confirmed (which doesn't make me any less of a Catholic according to official church doctrine, but does in the court of popular opinion); my knowledge of the Bible remains fragmentary. The relics prominently displayed in our home—multiple statues of the Blessed Virgin; the obligatory painting of the Last Supper; the torsioned, slightly glossy, and inevitably erotic hand-carved Jesus on the cross—were simply nods to our Filipinxness, for we had evolved past colonial thrall and become merely *cultural* Catholics.

Further padding my sense of entitlement was the presence of Lola (Tagalog for "grandmother"), who lived with my mother and me for most of the first twenty-seven years of my life. Mother and daughter had always had a fractious relationship, but whatever generosity Lola had failed to show her only child (one of my mother's many and oft-aired complaints) she certainly didn't fail to show her grandchild (to either compensate or make a point—I'm not sure which). So between my grandmother and mother (who was resolute about being exactly the kind of parent her own ostensibly unaffectionate mother wasn't), the coddling was ferocious. Under this heaving, sheltering matriarchy, I was safe.

(Is the narrator jettisoning complexity in favour of an overly quaint and therefore palatable narrative?)

April 30, 1984

> So last night I scored 90% and second place in the [piano] competition. Afterwards people came up to me and Mom and said I should have won. They said I was much more musical, played with much more feeling than the girl who won. I am furious, apoplectic—I practice so hard, wish so hard. I don't know what else to do.

Speaking mostly Tagalog at home and being brown didn't strike me as strange, living as we did in Vancouver's West End, which by the late 1970s had become a dense Babelian hotbed of multiple settler communities. (From preschool to grade twelve, I attended schools where white kids were the minority.) Culturally, however, Tagalog notwithstanding, our household was very white: virtually everything we watched on TV was white, and between the ages of five and ten, the music I most remember hearing was Judy Garland (whom my mother was fixated on) and ABBA (who, for better or worse, were just ubiquitous).

My mom and Lola seemed distinctly proud of two facts: their fair skin (Lola was a quarter Spanish, another fact they both seemed proud of), and that they hailed from Manila, or at least the general vicinity (Imus, Cavite, was only forty minutes away) and not, God forbid, the provinces (especially, for some reason, the Visayas). They weren't *bakya* (bumpkins), they told me; they had some privilege back home. Somehow, I grasped these as facts to hold on to, when in doubt.

So my early life was idyllic—and I was anxious to keep it that way. I think I was faintly aware that, like all paradisiacal illusions, it could rupture any second, and I remember being easily disquieted by anything or anyone that might precipitate that rupture. I developed an intense phobia of strangers—I would hide in my bedroom whenever we had guests and go into fits whenever a passerby on the street threw me what I interpreted as the evil eye. My mental space was my shelter, my sanctum; it would permit no aggression, no invasion, no rape.

July 6, 1984

> Mom had guests over tonight—a couple of white women from work. She forced me out of my room to play piano for them. It was horrible playing for these strangers, having them evaluate me, judge me. What do they know about music? Who do they think they are? And I'm upset at Mom for inviting them over without my permission. Anyways, I hate them. They think me a weirdo. That's because they are savages, with no feeling for the divine.

(By referring to the skin colour of his mother's friends, the boy is betraying a nascent awareness of his racialization.)

———————————

When pressed, most people, I think, can pinpoint the exact moment when their innocence ended, when heaven split away from earth, when things started to fall apart.

My rupture happened when I was in grade four.

The location: the playground. The time: morning recess.

I was sitting by the water fountain and a male classmate sat next to me.

"Do you play?" he asked cryptically.

"Play what?"

"You know, the gay way."

I knew what "gay" meant (I enjoyed watching *Three's Company*, lowbrow as it was—later, I would intellectualize my weakness for it by trumpeting its formal roots in Georges Feydeau and French farce). But I twigged to the unusual way the question and its explanation were phrased, in particular the deployment of that rhyming mnemonic. It was pointed, playful, gently malicious—and the first time such a question had been directed at me.

"*No!*"

I remember that *no* as welling from a place of utter horror. I was not *that*, could not be *that*. To be *that* was unspeakable, if not worse—much worse.

For it was 1985, and the world had just found out about AIDS. Put bluntly, to be *that* was just about the vilest thing one could be.

But I *was* that, and I knew it. I'd been flashlit, outed.

I'd always read a lot, but it was around this time that it became well-nigh compulsive.

The rupture had happened. I needed to cope.

It was one noon hour in the school library—where I usually hid during my lunch breaks—that I discovered L.M. Montgomery's *Anne of Green Gables*. The library's books, I remember, were alphabetized by title, so *Anne* was probably one of the first three or four books in the fiction section.

I connected instantly with the cover art for *Anne*: it was the famous 1942 edition with the young protagonist propped atop a heap of wood, enclosed in an oblong iris, which was in turn enclosed by rows of green and white abstractions that ably and efficiently suggested gables. I was drawn to Anne's plaintive looks—all old-soul, melancholy eyes. Her aching solitariness—underpinned by a bursting, indescribable sweetness—moved me, I remember, utterly.

That I was a boy reading a "book for girls" was not something that overly concerned me—at least, not enough to dissuade me from borrowing it. I probably did have a vague notion linking the liking of "girls'" things with that vile "way" in which I was accused of "playing": I remember being careful to read *Anne* only at home, and to never be seen reading or carrying it in school. But I also had enough chutzpah to be true to myself—I had no interest in G.I. Joe, or even boy-focused classic literature like *Huckleberry Finn*.

Anne saved my life, and that was that.

(Why doesn't the narrator go beyond scare quotes and interrogate why Anne of Green Gables *has been routinely pigeonholed as a "book for girls," not to mention why such a pigeonhole should even exist in the first place? Books like* Huckleberry Finn *and* Treasure Island *are rarely referred to as "books for boys," despite being as male-centric as* Anne *is female-centric.)*

———————————

There are the obvious reasons why a little brown queer boy would fall in love with Anne Shirley. Anne is an orphan and, consequently, like virtually every queer child, an outsider in every family she ends up with. With her red hair and freckles, she is, in her own way, racialized, given the still-present stigma against redheads in white society. She is a girl in a world that vastly prefers boys, shipped by mistake to a family expecting and wanting a boy. In the face of these challenges she strives, Herculean, towards unadulterated poetry, beauty, transcendence. This she achieves with her most unassailable attribute, her imagination, constructing a divine counterworld to the colonial conservatism of early-twentieth-century Prince Edward Island.

But even in the actual world, Anne—as her guardian Marilla would drily say—does well for herself. She transforms her fury at the world into a ferocious work ethic, leading to impressive academic and artistic achievements. She stands up to bullies who belittle her orphan status and red hair—can anyone resist cheering her epic takedown of the town busybody, Rachel Lynde? She's a feminist who stands up to and runs with the boys; her response to Gilbert Blythe is particularly admirable. Rather than crumble like Spanish shortbread before his good looks, she refuses to forgive him for the wrong he does her—he calls her "Carrots"—fiercely repudiating his advances for most of the book. Above all, she magically transforms her weaknesses into strengths, appropriating the stigmatized categories of *orphan girl* and *redhead* for her own triumphant individuation.

(*Shouldn't Voice Proper critique this disturbing early appropriation of female experience? It's perhaps fine at this early age for him to find empowerment in a female figure. But at some point he will have to discover the matrix in which Anne's story was conceived. For a boy to use a female figure for his own salvation is to reduce her—and by extent femaleness—to an instrument for his own personal development and unwittingly contribute to patriarchal erasure.*)

And, of course, there are the queer-tinged characters and relationships in the book. Anne's guardians, the elderly, unmarried brother-and-sister duumvirate of Matthew and Marilla, are qualified early in the book by Rachel Lynde as "a little odd." Gruff, angular, no-nonsense Marilla is emotionally guarded and uncomfortable with physical affection (she is "disturbed" by the "unaccustomedness and sweetness" of Anne's spontaneous caresses). Timid, taciturn Matthew is debilitatingly shy, especially around women, whom he dreads because of "an uncomfortable feeling that the mysterious creatures were secretly laughing at him." And Anne's "bosom" friendship with Diana is described in terms that are unambiguous and absolute in their devotion and passion. When Anne accidentally gets Diana drunk, and the latter's mother forbids their friendship to continue, Anne resorts to language worthy of Tennyson: "Fare thee well, my beloved friend. Henceforth we must be as strangers though we are living side by side. But my heart will ever be faithful to thee."

But looking back, it was another aspect of the book entirely that most entranced me—one easy to dismiss as merely "descriptive" that in fact carries all the novel's profundities: the presence of nature, which regularly bursts through the novel's interstices between its functional passages and Anne's overbearing, though lyrical, ramblings. It points to realities beyond what the book is allowed to contain, speaks truths beyond what the book is allowed to express. Sometimes its role as metaphor for a character's unconscious is obvious, as in the description of Marilla as not given to subjective analysis of her thoughts and feelings. She probably imagined that she was thinking about the Aids and the missionary box and the new carpet for the vestry room, but under these reflections was a harmonious consciousness of red folds smoking into pale-purply mists in the declining sun, of long, sharp-pointed fir shadows falling over the meadow beyond the brook, of still, crimson-bedded maples around a mirrorlike wood pall, of a wakening in the world and a stir of hidden pulses under the grey sod. The spring was abroad in the land, and Marilla's sober, middle-aged step was lighter and swifter because of its deep, primal gladness.

This ostensibly innocuous passage may be the most revelatory in the novel—apart from the allusions to genitalia and bodily fluids, the references to "Aids," "missionary," "box," and "sod" point to a collective erotic unconscious that is transhistorical and all-knowing (though the plurisignation of "sod" could possibly have been intentional—its gestation as British slang for "sodomite" occurred in the decade of L.M. Montgomery's birth). But more often in the book, nature is simply a divine aware presence, a Whitmanesque acknowledgment of sublime organic energies. It is the ultimate embodiment of the transcendence Anne strives for, of greatness and beauty that are eternal and absolute.

This portrayal had the effect of transporting me to another locale, to a lusher, more beautiful landscape than my own (yes, I'm from famously, incomparably beautiful British Columbia, which simply italicizes how discontent I was with my own reality and eager to be elsewhere).

(This extolling of nature seems a convenient default, a coded call to apoliticism and neutrality, because once grandiose, all-encompassing nature is invoked, further debate on anything suddenly becomes moot.)

The famous 1985 CBC television adaptation of *Anne of Green Gables* premiered shortly after I finished reading the book. I was unhappy with the way the miniseries reordered a number of the novel's scenes, and was disappointed that none of the actors spoke in British, or at least mid-Atlantic, accents (weren't all Canadians supposed to sound sort of British in those days?). Overall, though, I was captivated. We recorded the film the two nights it aired, which allowed me to watch it virtually every day for the next year. I would talk about it incessantly to the few friends I had at school, and find ways to mention it in every writing assignment I could. (Whatever stigma was attached to a boy openly liking this movie my obsession for it easily overrode.) And I loudly proclaimed my crush on Megan Follows, who played Anne—not exactly a lie (less about wanting her than wanting to *be* her) but more a pushback against the accusations being levelled against me than an honest declaration of lust.

For there was another aspect of the film whose peculiar energies were most preoccupying me. The moment Jonathan Crombie as Gilbert first appeared on the screen, the tenor of the film changed. Until that point, the world of Anne was cozily familiar, full of women and all the colours, textures, and modes associated with matriarchy. The sudden inflow of young male energy—so foreign and exotic to my eleven-year-old self—made for something darker, more menacing, more exciting—so exciting that, sometimes, unbeknownst to my working mother (but known to my non-working Lola, who didn't care, didn't tell, and would write me sick notes to take to school the next morning), I'd cut class and stay home, just to watch the movie, again and again.

Once, around this time, my father took my mother and me out for lunch. In his car afterwards, my mother, sitting in the passenger seat while I was in the back, told him that she'd heard me yelling the name "Gilbert" in my sleep in a manner not generally considered normative for a prepubescent boy. My father screeched the car to a halt, swung abruptly around, and smacked me hard in the face.

I blocked this incident out of my mind as soon as it happened and never dwelled on it again, until I started writing this book.

I've never asked my mother why she chose to divulge this information. I know it was out of genuine, if misguided, concern. As for my father's violence—even that I justified for the longest time: he's a product of his times, a macho, conservative Filipinx. Who could blame him for genuinely thinking he could beat the queer out of his son? Most fathers then thought that. Many still do.

For all my faults, holding grudges isn't one of them. My friends tell me repeatedly that I'm extremely forgiving.

(If he was a truly decolonized, progressive, self-respecting individual, he would see this as grounds for halting communication with his parents altogether.)

[Undated—circa summer 1986]

Oh, it's delightful to have ambitions. I'm so glad I have such a lot. And there never seems to be any end to them—that's the best of it. Just as soon as you attain one ambition, you see another one glittering higher up still. It does make life so interesting.

[—Anne of Green Gables]

[Undated—circa fall 1986]

The world calls them its singers and poets and artists and storytellers; but they are just people who have never forgotten the way to fairyland.

[—Anne of Green Gables]

June 27, 1986

It's been a week since I lost the Scholarship Prize to H. I am still crying myself to sleep. What makes H better than me? I know he's better at Math, but I'm better at Language Arts. I don't care that Miss K said she wanted to give it to both of us but that Mrs T [the school principal] told her she could only give it to one. Isn't that what they call "passing the buck"? That ONE should've been me. She made her choice and she blew it. Maybe she's still mad at me for putting the basketball in the garbage can a few months ago, but only because B told me to ...

Mom keeps saying, "Next time." I read that success is the sweetest revenge. So next time, revenge. If not, I will kill myself.

Anne saved my life. She entered my life exactly when I needed her; otherwise, I would have gone through the rupture completely alone. Her strength lit a fire under the part of me that remained intact, even as obsessiveness and anxiety started colonizing my young being. In her determination and triumph, I found hope.

Three decades later, shortly after his premature death of a brain hemorrhage, I read that Jonathan Crombie was queer, and that he didn't come out until his forties. At that moment, as I recalled the huge crush I had on him when I was a boy, an epiphanic shiver rushed up my spine.

2 | *ORDER:* A ROOM WITH A VIEW

When my obsession with *Anne of Green Gables* began to wane, I sought out books that were similar in theme and setting—period pieces with charismatic female misfits at their core: *Rebecca of Sunnybrook Farm, Little Women,* and *Pollyanna* were the most memorable of these post-Anne preoccupations. Then my tastes modernized and I turned to more contemporary novels that didn't trap women and girls in corsets and long dresses, such as *Up a Road Slowly* and *From Anna.*

It's worth discussing my virtually exclusive attraction to books about women and girls. Simply put, I saw—and felt—nothing of myself in stories about men and boys. Until the age of thirteen, I mostly disparaged them—my secret crushes on Jonathan Crombie and two handsome Czech classmates notwithstanding. I openly trashed boys as beneath me, though the subtext, admittedly, was both fear and envy that these boors possessed something important in their dispositions that I didn't. I found girls to be more interesting studies—more forthright emotionally, more advanced intellectually. And they seemed always to be vaguely struggling in ways boys didn't. I empathized with their struggles, though I couldn't yet name exactly what they were struggling against.

(He is dangerously close to romanticizing female oppression in this passage, and compromises his progressive aspirations by describing females as "studies." Does his status as a subaltern justify his appropriation of the stories of other subalterns, his empowerment at the expense of their erasure?)

My tastes shifted back to period pieces when, shortly after my twelfth birthday, I saw James Ivory's film adaptation of *A Room with a View.* I saw it with Lola—who was generous with money and always game for a movie—at a glorious, now long-defunct cinema complex in downtown Vancouver that housed ten tiny theatres and screened mostly art and independent films. I was struck by the film's poster—a young man and a young woman sitting facing each other in front of a window, his hand amorously on her cheek, and behind them quaint buildings clearly suggesting old Europe, enveloped from above by an enormous azure sky. It seemed highfalutin (I was ready for highfalutin). It was garnering glowing reviews, and I had begun to regard the approval of learned elites as the word of God and therefore blasphemous to ignore.

Lola didn't care for it—she thought it slow and "too full of old people" (highly debatable, given that only a few of the characters were elderly—but perhaps the British accents made everyone seem older than they were). I was lukewarm to it as well but felt obligated to like it, so with the steely inflexibility of a schoolmarm, I forced myself to like it, giving myself pep talks on how it was "art" and therefore good for me. They worked, for when the Oscars that year rolled around and *Room* lost best picture to *Platoon*, I was devastated. And indeed—setting aside Helena Bonham Carter's stilted performance—it's a lovely film, its highly proper, stiff-upper-lip surface pulsating with inner effervescence, passion, and joy.

So the film led me to the book (much as I hate to admit it, for a part of me has never surrendered the belief that it's intellectually lazy to take in an adaptation before reading the source material), and upon finishing it I felt catapulted to a different level of being—to the foot of a path leading straight to the peak of Mount Olympus. For E.M. Forster was a *real* author—meaning an author of books for grown-ups—and, as an undisputed member of the Western canon, a great one at that. Even more importantly, to my increasingly chaotic state of mind it offered an antidote: aesthetic perfection, Mozartean form and order.

The "Western canon" was a concept I discovered at precisely this time. (Allan Bloom's seminal, still fury-igniting book *The Closing of the American Mind* was published in 1987, the year I was transitioning from elementary to high school. No, I didn't read this famously erudite book at thirteen, but its shock waves could be felt even by an adolescent in [then] very provincial Vancouver. The book—revered by conservatives and loathed by progressives—is a fierce attack on the "politically correct" leftism that, in the author's view, encroached on American universities in the seventies and eighties, and an impassioned defence of "traditional learning" in general, and the Western canon in particular.)

Even before I knew what it signified, the term "Western canon" instantly intrigued me. Probably because I was desperately looking for empowerment at the time, I appreciated the assertive—even aggressive—connotations of "canon." And "Western" conjured up images of both macho cowboys (which both repulsed me as a non-macho queer boy and attracted me as a burgeoning, albeit mostly unwitting, misogynist) and the society I was taught from the outset to be grateful to belong to, because it was brilliant and advanced and unquestionably superior to any other. Upon discovering what the term meant, I pounced on it the way I would my bodybuilding program many years later: all I had to do was study the artworks that comprised this canon to be the best person I could possibly be.

Metaphor-switch: the Western canon was the canal I had to repeatedly cross to attain greatness. *A Room with a View* was my maiden voyage across it.

September 29, 1986

Transferred to Mr Z's class today.

Have been saved from the revolting, execrable, intolerable Hades that was Mr F's class.

Glory be to God

My final year of elementary school began badly when I found myself in the homeroom class of the disgusting Mr F. Mr F was a short, muscular, tattooed, motorcycle-riding, almost comically uber-masculine military man who, when he wasn't speaking in dulcet tones to his favourite girl-students, laboured obnoxiously under the delusion that his grade seven classroom was a wartime garrison. Mr F was the embodiment of what petrified me about men: he was simultaneously repulsive and threateningly erotic.

I would not be sidetracked in my pursuit of academic supremacy. I begged my mother to persuade the school hegemons to transfer me to Mr Z's mixed grade six/seven class, with the reason that I had more friends in the latter's class (a lie, for I had no friends anywhere).

My wish was granted (my "model pupil" reputation gave me clout). Mr Z was the polar opposite of Mr F. He was well dressed, quick-witted, sarcastic, and dramatic. The subjects he specialized in were creative writing and art. He was the most rigorous, most infuriating, most effective teacher I ever had. I despised him as much as I liked him. And, yes, he was queer.

I knew he was queer the second I met him (I had him for art the year prior). But although I was as homophobic as anyone—given my circumstances, probably more so—I felt safer with Mr Z than I ever did with Mr F. Mr Z may have been a homosexual, but at least he was an aesthete.

My first three months in Mr Z's class were the proverbial golden age of my scholastic career. My stories garnered me A-pluses and were read out regularly in class. With Napoleonic determination I conquered my Waterloo—math—by rehearsing my multiplication tables until they were part of my bloodstream. I scored (virtually) straight As on my report card (a B in PE, which I deemed too undignified an activity to count as a "real" course), and I attained school-wide acclaim as the resident pianist, amazing both teachers and students by playing mostly without scores, either by memory or by ear. I had never doubted my own brilliance, and Mr Z was validating it. The recognition I so badly wanted was finally, indisputably mine.

But after Christmas break, something shifted in our relationship. He became more cursory and less patient with me. He'd pick on me to answer questions in class and berate me for "not participating" (I detested "class participation"—I convinced myself that it was a collectivist activity and therefore beneath me; in actuality, I suffered from debilitating shyness and abject fear of exposure). Looking back, I still contend that Mr Z was unnecessarily mean to me, though I understand why—in me he probably saw something of his younger self, and was triggered.

As for me, the daily exposure to embodied, flesh-and-blood queerness—in the form, no less, of the primary authority figure in my life outside of my home—wreaked havoc on my conflicted, confused subconscious. During this time I acted out in ways I am profoundly ashamed of, via vicious and terrifying explosions of bigotry.

January 17, 1987

> *I'm flabbergasted—absolutely flabbergasted—that N tied with me for top marks on the math test. Since when did Natives ever excel in school? Aren't they all born with Foetal Alcohol Syndrome? Isn't that supposed to retard their intellectual development?*

One day around this time a man brushed past me at the mall, nearly knocking me down. He was obviously in a rush and also, I sensed—from the way he walked—queer. Annoyed at this disregard for my body, and further annoyed by the presumed identity of the one doing this disregarding, I cried, completely without thinking, "Oh, God, I'm gonna get AIDS!" The man didn't hear, but another pair of men—who I also sensed were queer—looked back at me, then barked at each other, "Fuck, what a little asshole."

All I can say is that at that moment, I was a living toilet for bigotry—stupidly, barbarically young, unquestioningly flushing up society's collective hate. Indeed, I believe that every gesture I've made as an adult towards social justice has been in some way an attempt to live down this horrible moment from my youth.

March 10, 1987

> *I will not get AIDS; if I do I will kill myself.*
> *I will not get AIDS; if I do I will kill myself.*
> *I will not get AIDS; if I do I will kill myself.*
> *I will not get AIDS; if I do I will kill myself.*
> *I will not get AIDS; if I do I will kill myself.*
> *I will not get AIDS; if I do I will kill myself.*
> *I will not get AIDS; if I do I will kill myself.*
> *I will not get AIDS; if I do I will kill myself.*

My fear of AIDS—which began virtually as soon as I first heard about it a couple of years prior—had by this point evolved into something near pathological. I experienced heart palpitations in music class, convinced that the virus was living on the recorders we played on. Predictably, public restrooms became bona fide *bêtes noires*, as did handshakes, hugs, glasses, and utensils.

Even though it had been firmly established that AIDS could not spread via casual contact, my narcissism convinced me that I would somehow be the exception, that early death would be the price for my prodigious intelligence and talent. But this narcissism, as always, contained a shadow side that was self-hating: AIDS, I believed, was the punishment that would befall me for being who, deep down, I already knew I was.

I developed a ritual wherein each time I washed my hands, I'd wash them eight times. It was my ward against illness and evil, my guarantor for the realization of my ambitions. I settled on the number eight because it connoted musical symmetry, and the two circles that are its visual symbol implied stasis and self-completion.

With this and other rituals (tapping the doorknob eight times before leaving the house, adding the ultimatum of killing myself to every wish I wanted actualized), I was determined to maintain a sense of order in my life. I felt that by performing these rituals I could remain at least partially above ground, above the quicksand that threatened to engulf me.

To stumble upon *A Room with a View* at this point in my life was, like discovering *Anne* when I did, a godsend. Just when my mind began, in earnest, what would turn out to be a lifelong struggle with chaos, *Room* provided me with a semblance of its opposite, in the form of orderly, classically proportioned, joyful literature.

[Undated—circa March 1987]

Things to do tomorrow:

Gurgle mouth 8 x

Listen to 8 of Bach's preludes and fugues to make your mind as brilliant as it can possibly be

Practice piano

Wash hair 8 x

Practice multiplication tables 8 x

Practice world capitals 8 x

Practice table of elements 8 x

Continue reading Great Expectations

April 15, 1987

Mom told me she had a horrible, abysmal nightmare the other night about how she had to call the police because Mr Z abducted me. I asked her why she had this dream. "Why does anyone dream what they dream?" she said.

She made me promise not to go with Mr Z anywhere outside of school. As if that would ever happen. I hate him.

July 7, 1993

[about my classmate Jan]

Next row over

A little in front of me

His sleeveless taut arms

Untie this knot

Project Partner

It's like I belong

No longer Genius

No longer Fairy

He calls me Friend

And finally merry

For knot is untied

If ever so slightly

Weeks later his birthday

I write him a card

Sentences crafted & sculpted

& pretty

But goes unacknowledged

And gaze avoided

The knot tied back

Tightly, tightly

For a cluster of reasons, *A Room with a View*—the story of the sexual, intellectual, and emotional awakening of Lucy Honeychurch—is the literary work whose practical, real-life impact on me has been the most pronounced. To this day, I return to it in moments of doubt and duress.

To match the tone of my anxious, academically rigorous twelve-year-old self, I will present the reasons for *Room*'s impact on me as a list—a form that I was quite fond of as a child, for it offered little stays of order against complete mental chaos.

1. *Its relevant tensions.* The Middle Ages and the Renaissance, the mind and the body, Christianity and paganism, the upper classes and the lower. These are the various forms of the novel's yin and yang, intellectually vigorous yet embedded beautifully in character and action. Conformity and liberation battle for the soul of our young Everywoman, but the battle—though no doubt tortuous for the character—is presented by the author with such a gentle touch that, contrary to being repelled by it, we wish to undergo it ourselves, to be, with Lucy, on the battlefield on which this existential duel takes place. For this gentleness has the paradoxical effect of *inviting us in*—to see for ourselves how essential this battle is to our spiritual growth. (Indeed, of the twentieth century's truly great authors, Forster, with his liberal humanism and quiet, self-effacing style, is by far the most infinitely likeable.) To this day, the novel divides my loyalties:

although my erotic attraction is to the working-class, masculine, impulsive George Emerson—who represents what the novel names the "Renaissance" ideals of passion, authenticity, and free-spiritedness—my sympathies remain strong for the man Lucy rejects for George, the repressed Cecil Vyse—stand-in for priggish conformity masquerading as culturedness. For all his book learning, Cecil is "medieval": he is snarky, supercilious, pretentious, infuriating—but he is me. He was me at twelve and is still partially me today. A part of me would have preferred to see Lucy choose Cecil, or join "the vast armies of the benighted" and become a spinster (although I have come to embrace hedonism, I have residual respect for the virtues and benefits of self-denial.) At twelve, though, I was probably hoping that Lucy would remain just as miserable as I was; however, that she didn't gave me hope for my own future. More important was Lucy's maturation from passive ingenue to self-assured young woman—as enmeshed as I was in my twelve-year-old paranoias, I still recognized that Lucy's transformation was something to aspire to.

2. *Its formal beauty.* The tautness and efficiency; the cold classicism of its bipartite structure; the meaningful, considered allusions to Greek and Roman mythology; the meaningful, considered references to Giotto and Leonardo, Beethoven and Schumann. After reading the book, I felt edified by a hard certainty: this is what a work of literature should look like—symmetrical in form, understated in tone, and replete with references to the culture that birthed it. That the culture in question is as hegemonic as it is majestic must be acknowledged; still, we must always affirm—in the noble tradition of our queer forebears Pater, Symonds, and Wilde—our right to pleasure. As a twelve-year-old hypochondriac who thought daily about death and erasure, I clung as if for dear life to *Room*'s marmoreal beauty as artifice.

3. *Its imparting of joy.* But above all is something happily less pedantic. *Room* is a work of serious literature that oozes irrepressible joy—in both life and living, in both the destination and the journey. When I think of *A Room with a View*, I think of air and sky—the colour blue predominates, the colour of communication, and of the divine. If I resort to mysticism it is because Forster's art is therewith touched; at twelve, I hungered for the divine; and *Room* fed it to me.

(Numerous problems here. First, Voice Proper waxes enthusiastic about the novel's ending without acknowledging that it hits a distinctly anti-feminist note, with Lucy's "salvation" gained via a romantic relationship with a man. A more empowering ending would have allowed Lucy to be courageously alone—as it stands, Forster caves in to the narrative pressure to sentimentalize. And why wouldn't he? The enduring popularity of his novels—and the films made of them—is ample proof that Forster, inadvertently and despite his good intentions, aligned ultimately with the status quo, diffidently yet persuasively arguing that if we "only connect," we can diminish injustice.

As for pleasure—to claim the right to it is less admirable defiance than truistic posturing. Voice Proper is welcome to pleasure, but let's not pretend it's never at someone else's expense. The lower-class Emersons, for example, are little more than noble savages, and the treatment of southern Europeans is pornographic fetishization. No need to elaborate on the most ostentatious problem: this racialized intellectual cites this whitest of white books as his greatest influence. And again, like the depiction of nature, the invocation of joy is a discourse-ender, a hegemonic attempt to stifle further politicizing. For what can possibly be political about joy?)

Although grade seven was an academic triumph for me, it ended on a sombre note. My relationship with Mr Z had deteriorated badly. Piano competitions took me out of school for much of the spring, which my displeased teacher used to justify continuing to pick on me. To my consternation, he gave me two fewer As on my third-term report card. The topper came when, in the middle of summer, a social worker materialized on our doorstep, for Mr Z had told authorities that I was worrisomely anti-social. The ensuing plan was to have me participate in activities with a bunch of other similarly challenged kids, but the worker backed off (I think my piano-playing entranced her—music is always convenient at times like this, as though musical talent explains and justifies anti-social tendencies). That incident solidified my enmity towards Mr Z; for despite all his good intentions, he had deployed the state apparatus to tame me. I've never been able to forgive him.

Later that summer, I was strolling down Robson Street—downtown Vancouver's primary shopping thoroughfare—with Mom and Lola, and we saw Mr Z arranging clothes outside the store where he held a summer job. After we exchanged pleasantries and said goodbye, Mom and Lola burst into uncontrollable laughter. *"Baklang baklang naman,"* they managed between guffaws. (Translation: What a faggot.) With strident enthusiasm, I joined in. After all, I'd just finished reading Great Literature; I was feeling good about myself, and mocking Mr Z intensified that feeling.

When September arrived, I was in high school. Still heavily under the influence of *Room*, I started affecting a British accent. I also started telling people that I came from a wealthy family, figuring it was harmless to forge a fake identity for myself. I'd been accepted to an academically renowned high school on the opposite side of the city from where I lived, so I knew nobody. Plus, I wanted to fit in with the school's affluent demographic, situated as it was in one of Vancouver's richest neighbourhoods.

The British accent phase was over as soon as a passerby on the street yelled at me to shut up. The wealthy family schtick was put to rest as soon as my schoolmates found out that I couldn't go to Acapulco for spring break like the rest of them.

October 22, 1987

I walked in on Mom kissing [her boyfriend] L just now.

So I've run and come to YOU, the one safe space in this world.

Around this time, I found out E.M. Forster was queer. (*Maurice*, his only explicitly queer-themed novel, was published after his death.) A strange sensation came over me—I felt weak-kneed and ill, as queerness was inextricably linked in my mind with AIDS. But it was also as though something above me had opened and there was suddenly light shining on something that had always been half in shadow.

At once, I felt both afflicted and less alone.

3 | *RETREAT:* A STREETCAR NAMED DESIRE

At thirteen, I woke up and began feeling, if not yet completely living, in my body. That's what happened when I first encountered Tennessee Williams's play *A Streetcar Named Desire*.

May 5, 1987

> Spent seven hours again today practicing. After not a single first-place finish at the festival I must do everything to ensure only victories at the next one. Spent two and a half hours on Bach, two and a half on Beethoven, two on Chopin, who comes to me more easily as he is soft and frail like me; but Bach and Beethoven, whom I admire more, I must work on—they are subtler yet more solid, marmoreal, exposed. While practicing the second movement of the Italian Concerto today, my eyes were closed and for two seconds I saw God. So this is why I play the piano—thank you, God, for reminding me.

(*This Filipinx queer boy's single-minded focus on Western high art affirms and perpetuates familiar hegemonies.*)

My first exposure to *Streetcar* was not the 1951 Vivien Leigh–Marlon Brando film version but the far less heralded 1984 television adaptation starring Ann-Margret and Treat Williams.

What I most remember from the film was the heat. The heat of a world of inverted values, where unadulterated physicality assumed absolute primacy. Of unapologetic, brutal, sweat-soaked masculinity. Of words slipping and sliding against one another with poetic abandon.

Complete innocence was just behind me, and I was at the threshold of awareness. I wasn't yet able to put words to my feelings, but *Streetcar* seemed to speak them for me.

It would be too obvious—and not quite accurate—to write about how Stanley Kowalski ignited lust in me (though he did), or how in his dainty, ethereal sister-in-law Blanche DuBois I saw a reflection of myself (though I did). At thirteen, I wasn't yet able to be completely honest with myself on those fronts. My identification with *Streetcar* was at once more miasmic and visceral, hitting my very core, addressing truths I wasn't yet ready to confront. In the end, I had no choice but to retreat.

October 8, 1987

I caught Mom kissing L again.

Yesterday I overheard her talking on the phone with C [her friend] about how L is the love of her life.

Tonight L talked about taking all of us back to La Mancha with him, where he's from.

"Isn't La Mancha where Don Quixote's from?" I ask.

He smiles, pats my shoulder, tells me I'm bright.

I was discovering I could access the transcendence I had previously accessed through art, through the body. *Streetcar* helped me make this discovery, as did my mother's boyfriend, and a boy in school. But it was a discovery I wasn't ready for, forcing me to retreat into the safety of my mind.

I was engaged in a duel between two distinct versions of self. To borrow from psychoanalyst Jacques Lacan's theory of the mirror stage, there was my actual, bodily self—awkward, gawky, and, quite possibly, I was starting to sense, deviant—and the self I saw reflected in my piano-playing and writing—adroit, high-minded, coherent.

This clash I saw reflected in *Streetcar*. Blanche DuBois, as nuanced and conflicted a heroine as any created by Sophocles or Shakespeare, clings to the rarefied virtues of chivalry and high art while wrestling with her hungering, demonic animal self. She lays out her ideology in her famous scene 4 monologue, in which she warns her sister about Stanley:

> He acts like an animal, has an animal's habits! Eats like one, moves like one, talks like one! There's even something—sub-human—about him—something not quite at the stage of humanity yet! Yes, something—ape-like about him, like one of those pictures I've seen in—anthropological studies! Thousands and thousands of years have passed him right by and there he is—Stanley Kowalski—survivor of the Stone Age! Bearing the raw meat home from the kill in the jungle! And you—you here, waiting for him! ... Maybe we are a long way from being made in God's image, but Stella—my sister—there has been some progress since then! Such things as art—as poetry and music—such kinds of new light have come into the world since then! In some kinds of people some tenderer feelings have had some little beginning! That we have got to make grow! And cling to and hold as our flag! In this dark march toward whatever it is we're approaching ... Don't—don't hang back with the brutes!

Unfortunately, this beautiful monologue, which springs from the profoundest wells of Blanche's spirit and sense of life, is too often played for facile laughs, an opportunity for audiences, which are largely, at least in North America, democratic and anti-elitist, to snicker at a pretentious and uppity woman. (Of all the Blanches I've seen only Vivien Leigh—appropriately enough, a Brit—delivers it with the necessary soulful sincerity.) In fact, this monologue is an impassioned apologia for high culture, and as a burgeoning artist/aesthete/queer man, high culture was something I could easily get behind. At thirteen, I already knew there was an incontestable link between queers and art, and although I couldn't yet identify as queer, I was ready to identify as an artist.

As an artist, therefore, I would only align, *could* only align with the rarefied, the singular, the difficult. "Superior things! Things of the mind and the spirit!" exclaims Amanda Wingfield in *The Glass Menagerie*, another of Tennessee Williams's transcendence-seeking Southern Gothics. During a discussion on crime in my high school law class, I haughtily offered my lack of sympathy for those who committed violence in self-defence: "Instincts are for animals,"

I said, paraphrasing another of Amanda's lines—an opinion that was roundly sneered at. But I was unrepentant—because I had successfully convinced myself that I was a prince among peasants, my attitude towards my schoolmates was one of unalloyed disdain.

My politics were aligning with my fierce individualism. I was imbibing the mutterings of Ayn Rand and identifying as an objectivist—a follower of her philosophy that stresses reason-based, heroic individualism (I hadn't yet happened upon her racist and homophobic views, but neither had I come out to myself, so I doubt it would have made much difference). Later, I would read Plato's *Republic* and the writings of Edmund Burke and identify my politics as firmly right-of-centre, aligning against what I perceived to be the gutter mentality that flourished under the rubric of "democracy." And I would take to heart Yukio Mishima's advice that homosexuals always support the right, for they have everything to lose from majority rule, as the majority will always be homophobic. (For reasons that were yet unknown to me this dictum stuck.) At my loopiest I declared that although fascism was an undesirable extreme, its sense of form and proportion was at least aesthetically beautiful. I was a self-hating conservative, clinging to any sense of established order to keep a lid on my burgeoning passions.

July 25, 1988

Hottest day of the summer so far. I sit upright at my desk in an effort to get away.

The heat, the garish sun, those bodies—revolting.

It should be illegal for people to take their shirts off in public. It is an unnecessary hindrance, an infelicitous roadblock on the path to one's sole and proper objective: intellectual elevation.

March 21, 1988

There is nothing more beautiful than E. Today in French class I was given his quiz to mark. Typical dumb jock—he scored 2 out of 10. When I gave him back his quiz he said, "I know, I'm a total lame-o. Embarrassing. Thanks dude." I caught a glimpse of his blue eyes—they radiate kindness, something I had never seen before in any male—those linear, solipsistic creatures, as fascistic and indifferent as fate. But today the plaster cracked; in the face of E, Adonis incarnate. A new paradigm, exemplar, for everything I want to be.

Blanche DuBois's stature in queer male culture is unquestioned. Queer men will call each other Blanche in moments of teasing, gentle censure; her most famous lines are fixtures in the cultivated queer man's repartee bank; she figures in works as diverse as *All about My Mother* and *The Golden Girls*. The oft-iterated deconstruction of Blanche as a queer man in drag is too crass, if not wholly inaccurate. A more precise explanation for her popularity is that Blanche makes the suffering of queer men visible, that she suffers for us, that the path of debasement she travels is actually our own.

(The narrator should deploy the term "gay" rather than "queer." Most sexually nonconforming men either have never heard of or have no interest whatsoever in Blanche DuBois.)

Yet Blanche is a homophobe. She marries a closeted young poet named Allan who's possessed of "a nervousness, a softness and tenderness which wasn't like a man's." He comes to her "for help": "He was in the quicksands and clutching at me, but I wasn't holding him out, I was slipping in with him!" She exposes him after she walks in on him with a man: "I saw—I know—you disgust me," she says, her words reverberating with the weight of centuries of heterosexist bigotry. He then sticks a revolver fellatio-style in his mouth and blows his head off, following the classic triadic sequence of homosexual immolation: consummation, exposure, suicide.

But Blanche gets her comeuppance. Indeed, with a classical symmetry that gives *Streetcar* the rightness and inevitability of Greek tragedy, her downfall matches Allan's step for terrifying step. Just as Allan tried to play it straight, Blanche attempts to play it prim, sweeping her dissolute past beneath a veneer of hyper-ladylike gentility. Her numerous illicit affairs are discovered then brutally exposed by both the effeminate Mitch and the thuggish Stanley. Both attempt to rape her; Stanley succeeds and drives her to madness, her mental death a direct analogue to Allan's physical one. In the end, Blanche retreats to the one safe space available to the homosexual: the beauty-laden, reality-altering confines of the mind.

As for Stanley Kowalski, he provides an occasion, in these socio-politically volatile times, for non-dualistic thinking. He is opposed to virtually everything I have extolled and elevated my entire life; nonetheless, vile as he is, he has my partial affection. I see him as the scrappy, ambitious child of Polish immigrants, he is a forthright working-class husband and expectant father making do in an economic system not of his choosing. The very real threat posed by his aristocratic sister-in-law explains, if not justifies, his crassness and brutality; beneath the hyper-macho pyrotechnics is abject fear.

As for Stanley's beauty—so indelibly embodied by both Marlon Brando and Treat Williams—it proves, for the character, a double-edged sword. Sex being the great equalizer, it levels the playing field between him and Blanche: pulling her down to his level, he reduces her to an animal. But ultimately it works against him, facilitates his eventual emasculation, for he's reduced to a sex symbol, still lusted after, to this day, (at least as embodied by the young Brando, perhaps the first real male sex symbol in Western pop culture) by the very demographic—male homosexuals—Blanche stands in for. *As Stanley himself objectified, he, in turn, is objectified.* Blanche has her triumph. The circle is complete.

(Treat Williams's Stanley Kowalski was the first person this boy masturbated to, the boy being the penetrator in the fantasized scenario. In hindsight, he may have subconsciously been retaliating on Blanche's behalf.)

April 20, 1990

[poem about L]

When he touches my mother
I touch him
Bliss knows no division
no boundary
no law

The greatness of *Streetcar* lies in the parity, the equal attention it gives to the duelling sides of our binaries—the spirit and the flesh, the constructed and the chthonic, Apollo and Dionysus, art and ardour. Art is manifest in Blanche's florid sentences, her tragically tawdry finery, her moth-like, flutteringly defiant stand against what she calls "deliberate cruelty." The New Orleans of the play is a den of lustful, ravenous Darwinism; she suffers her various indignities like a sheet-white relic of Old World gentility, all the while uttering some of the sublimest lines in American dramatic literature. But this lustful, ravenous Darwinism is given more than its due, suffusing Blanche DuBois in a thrillingly Boschian polychromaticism. Brawny, brutal, roughhousing poker players; sweat-soaked street vendors and mantra-chanting Mexican flower ladies; a fecund young wife and her beautiful, virile husband, igniting coloured lights with their insatiable fucking. The central conflict in the play, that between Blanche and Stanley, is all the more wrenching because, to a degree, it is also a mating dance. Blanche is as drawn to Stanley as she is repulsed by him; therein lies the texturedness of their encounters.

But at the end, and above everything else, metatheatrically transcending the sordid proceedings like some divine reminding presence, is the play as a work of art, as technically seamless as any ever written. Its architectural ingenuity—how Blanche's destruction is a structural echo of her dead husband's. Its dazzling surface—the plethora of poetic imagery, the purposeful mythological allusions to Philomela, Procne, Tereus, interlocking, interweaving, simultaneously deepening and elevating. Its masterful aurality—the two lead characters' disparate semantic structures conjoining in a dissonant harmony, like some inexplicably pitch-perfect hybrid of Mozart and Schoenberg. It is a work of beauty, aching in its formal finish, triumphant and all-redeeming.

(There's something unethical—amoral—about this New Critical exaltation of form, something cowardly, snail-like, like Nero fiddling while Rome burned. Voice Proper waxing ecstatic about aesthetic beauty in the face of rape, spousal abuse, mental illness, family betrayal, and institutionalization shows his reluctance to wholly relinquish the conservatism of his youth. And the ambiguity with which he

infuses Blanche's rape by calling it "also a mating dance" must be unequivocally rejected: rape is always only an unjustifiable act of violence.)

[Undated—circa spring 1988]

Darkness
Bleeds in
Through the white walls
Of my raped mind

The mind—still the place I retreat to when times get tough. My escapes have never been via alcohol or drugs but by retreating completely from external reality and into the grimly gnostic crevices of my mind.

Streetcar's influence on me was profound, forcing to the surface erotic energies I wasn't yet prepared to wholly face—except in the realm of writing, which, in my mid-teens, was where I directed *all* of my life energy. The stories I produced in high school, teeming with sex and violence, were invariably florid meditations on the profane and the visceral. But they were also—perhaps strangely, given my sympathy and love for Blanche DuBois—misogynist (or perhaps not so strange at all: both art and life have shown me how misogyny is sometimes the shadow side of male homosexuality). One story had the heroine bludgeon her own vagina with a knife; in another, a seamstress sewed hers closed. In both, the female protagonists functioned as my surrogates: like E.M. Forster and Tennessee Williams, I could only project myself onto female characters. There was, of course, the very real threat of homophobia, which made writing openly about queer realities virtually impossible. But looking back, I don't see that as a good enough reason to subject female characters—and female readers—to such horrors. A necessary phase in my creative growth, perhaps—I needed to get these sensationalistic impulses out of my system in order to arrive at a subtler writing style—as well as my personal well-being—my erotic energies needed *some* outlet to keep me in reasonably good mental health—but I regret the damage to others I may have caused.

That my relationship to women has been, and is, complex might be understandable given they were always the dominant gender in my personal life. They held the power, demanded the respect—a proven recipe for contempt. But they were also my only links to the "real" world, so to speak—the world beyond my backwater where nothing ever happened except art and literature.

Lola in particular was a grounding and enlightening influence on me. Much calmer than my mother, she was a steadying force in our otherwise manic household. I was in my mid-teens when she opened up to me—matter-of-factly, without sentimentality, and with even some of her trademark dry humour peppered in—about her life in the Philippines during World War II, the struggles her family underwent during the Japanese occupation (under which almost a million Filipinx people died), and the traumatic events she witnessed firsthand—namely, the rape of a number of her friends by both Japanese and American soldiers. This was the only bit of Filipinx history I ever learned growing up. Lola was also the only person I spoke Tagalog with regularly, so whatever Tagalog I still possess, I owe almost completely to her. Besides my brown skin (which still occasionally causes strangers to speak slow, extra-enunciated English to me), my Tagalog—as fragmentary as it is—is often the only thing I have to remind me that I'm not white.

(Good that he knows at least a bit of Filipinx history. But does he know how successful Filipinx resistance to the occupation actually was? So much so that by war's end, Japan controlled only twenty-five percent of the country. Filipinx history goes far beyond victimhood.)

April 6, 1988

E has stopped saying hi to me. Up 'til last week he'd say hello whenever he saw me. Then he caught me staring at him.

I was staring at him on purpose. I thought we had a connection.

He hollered, "Do you have a problem?" I was frozen, speechless. He rolled his eyes and stormed away.

Obviously I have a problem. One of the few boys who I thought was different is just *as godforsaken, as vile, as plebeian as the rest of them. He ignores me, looks right past me. I will retaliate, he will do right by me. If not I will kill myself.*

I stepped outside my head. The results were disappointing.

Upon seeing *Streetcar*, I came out to myself—formally, officially, with the bushy-tailed, starry-eyed obdurateness of a postulant nun—as an artist. I wanted entry into Art's inviolable order. Within its confines I would be safe.

Blanche DuBois—the romantic idealist who defied repugnant, brute reality—became my patron saint. I came to see her fate not as oversensitivity, not as insanity, but rather as self-removal from the philistinism of the earth below.

(A Streetcar Named Desire *is not about Blanche DuBois; it is about Allan Gray.*

The play's characters are all fragments of the character Allan w/should have been. Every character is an imposter, taking space away from what w/should be Allan's.

Tennessee Williams denied him stage life—denied him appearance, body, voice.

One of the pre-eminent queer playwrights of the twentieth century was complicit in his kind's own minimization.)

The discovery that Tennessee Williams, like E.M. Forster, was queer, was all the proof I needed to confirm the existence of a race of people defined by both homosexuality and artistic genius.

4 | *GEIST:* DEATH IN VENICE

If *A Streetcar Named Desire* gives tangible form to carnal desire, *Death in Venice* goes a step further and reifies—explicitly, without disguise or sublimation—*queer* carnal desire and, most pertinent for me, its relation to art, and how it motors one, with feverish intensity, towards geist.

Geist, nobility of mind and thought, transcendence—the aims of modernist art, early-twentieth-century religious occultism, bohemian love. The flight to the sun frenetically, almost wilfully innocent.

June 29, 1992

Last day of school. Last day of high school. Last day of being around unbridled, enabled savagery. These sweat-soaked boys with their brawn and tank tops, who've shunned me, snickered at me these last five years—up my sleeve is retribution which I will unfurl as soon as today ends, the only way I know how: as an artist.

I will scour the world clean of its intellectual and emotional detritus, the flotsam of abortive humanity. I will impale the human race on the sword of its own shame, a sword come to life by my mimetic genius. I will rape the cesspool that masquerades as society, this infected and infecting womb for never-ending spiritual ineptitude.

In high school I was a priest among mobsters—so I thought—a frail, quivering wisp of divinity among apes. University was the promised land, where I would no longer need to tiptoe, where I would breathe in the legacy of the Academy, of Alexandria, of Clonmacnoise, where the spirits of my intellectual fathers would at long last be living presences, where the higher love that was my birthright would suffuse me, keep me safe.

Higher love. In AIDS, Chaos had morphed from Miltonian construct to tangible reality, had taken terrifying form as fatal, shameful disease. Higher love had become life jacket, life rope, salvation. Higher love was no longer edifying accoutrement but stark necessity.

That I read *Death in Venice* while still in the grip of AIDS phobia made the experience as unbearable as it was enthralling. As a young adult inevitably immersed in the idea—if not yet the practice—of sex, I received the book in a matrix of high anxiety and transcendental straining. At eighteen, the abyss was no longer metaphor but immovable, gaping fact. *Death in Venice* was at once gospel aria and grisly documentary.

For any nebbishy young aesthete for whom nothing ever happens except art and literature, the story is achingly, agonizingly personal. Gustav von Aschenbach, an aging writer of repute, heads to Venice in an effort to relieve himself of writer's block. Shortly after arriving he encounters a staggeringly beautiful adolescent named Tadzio. Aschenbach is awestruck. With ever-increasing obsessiveness, but without exchanging a single word with him, he follows the boy around, while his exquisite, assiduously constructed inner world slowly crumbles. Finally, stricken by the cholera epidemic sweeping the city, Aschenbach expires on the beach whilst gazing at his beloved.

Higher love. So as an AIDS-era queer boy I embraced a secular Puritanism, railing against the hubristic freedom of go-with-the-flow carnality. My life, I decided, would be one of unyielding formalist rigour: flawlessly executed diurnal routines, exquisitely sculpted sentences. I would die with absolute supremacy over my person tragically intact, sacrificing mortal joys to wage a lifelong battle against imperfection.

February 12, 1993

Had German Studies today. Discussed Death in Venice. *Apollo and Dionysus, art and ardour. The familiar binaries harder, more petrified, more indissoluble. Two days before Valentine's and everywhere around me is love—lower love, base love, love bestial and not exquisite. I am so firmly Apolline that I feel not an ounce of frustration, but neither am I edified by any self-congratulatory pride. All I feel, in every region of me, is dead.*

Death in Venice is ribboned with imperious odes to spiritual straining, to unflinching self-discipline, to radical, unbending will. Above all, it's a morality play about resistance to the now and indomitable commitment to the not-now. Its Everyman, Aschenbach, is, despite being a great writer, fairly ordinary, so the reader's identification with him is appropriately straightforward and simple. Shouldering, it seems, the weight of the entirety of European civilization ("too preoccupied with the tasks imposed upon him by his own sensibility and by the collective European psyche"), Aschenbach "was the writer who spoke for all those who work on the brink of exhaustion ... those moralists of achievement who are slight of nature and scanty of resources, but who yet by some ecstasy of the will and by wise husbandry, manage at least for a time to force their work into a semblance of greatness." Like Blanche DuBois, Gustav von Aschenbach suffers for sensitive, artistically inclined queers.

Ecstasy of the will, semblance of greatness—the novella's true setting is not Venice but the torturous, never-ending staircase of the creative life:

> They were not broad, the shoulders which carried the tasks laid upon him by his talent; and since his aims were high, he stood in great need of discipline ... Aschenbach would begin his day early by dashing cold water over his chest and back and then, with two tall wax candles in silver candlesticks placed at the head of his manuscript, he would offer up to art, for two or three ardently conscientious morning hours, the strength he had gathered during sleep. It was a pardonable error, indeed it was one that betokened as nothing else could the triumph of the moral will, that uninformed critics should mistake [his work] for the product of solid strength and long stamina, whereas in fact they had built up their impressive size from layer upon layer of daily opuscula, from a hundred or thousand separate inspirations.

The novella is also replete with profound reflections on the nature of art, including this statement (particularly relevant to me at the time, as I had just started reading Pater, Symonds, and Wilde, all ardent apologists for "art for art's sake") on the moral ambivalence of form:

Has not form two aspects? Is it not moral and immoral at once: moral in so far as it is the expression and result of discipline, immoral—yes, actually hostile to morality—in that of its very essence it is indifferent to good and evil, and deliberately concerned to make the moral world stop beneath its proud and undivided sceptre?

(His preoccupation with form and aesthetics is yet another expression of his internalized white supremacy.)

Beauty. Form. Art for art's sake. The philosophical line of Pater, Symonds, and Wilde ends tragically in this novella, published just two years before World War I destroyed virtually all pretense of the sustainability of apoliticism. (Complete destruction had to wait until World War II.) Aschenbach's concern for form verges on the absolute, as evidenced by his repeated objectification of Tadzio:

> With astonishment Aschenbach noticed the boy was entirely beautiful. His countenance, pale and gracefully reserved, was surrounded by ringlets of honey-colored hair, and, with its straight nose, its enchanting mouth, its expression of sweet and divine gravity, it recalled Greek sculpture of the noblest period; yet despite the purest formal perfection, it had such a unique personal charm that he who now contemplated it felt he had never beheld, in nature or in art, anything so consummately successful.

March 2, 1993

G IS PRESENCE. In German studies class last week he sits beside me and I can't breathe, because he jolts me into presence when I function better elsewhere—in the transcendent, rarefied safety of the defiant not-now. He finds the tiny cracks in my armour of virtue and floods them with the ENERGY of the force-field of his physicality: his magnificent height, his glistening brawn, his long, dirty-blond locks, his stabbing blue eyes. He sits beside me and he's imposing, he is sensitive, he is perspicacious—in mellifluous tones he expounds on how, just as love and hate are actually two sides of a single coin and therefore flip with great ease into each other, Germany's arduous, Icarus-like ascent to the heavens (i.e., literature, philosophy, music) could only, inevitably, collapse into barbarism (to wit, Nazism). His energy becomes mine and I am paralyzed, shocked—until I remember higher love and ease back to sanity.

(His worship of this white man is automatic, inevitable—yet in his naming of the man's "dirty-blond locks" and "blue eyes," as well as his use of the weaponized descriptor "stabbing," lie seeds, possibly, of a future willingness to denormalize whiteness.)

Objectification, intellectualization, distancing—Aschenbach clings to these methods like a man caught in quicksand, to the vines of a dying tree, one planted and therefore unnatural. From resplendent discreteness to chaotic, chthonic oneness—the fall is fluttering, graceless, pathetic, concomitant with the cholera epidemic hurtling from, of course, the "primitive" East, that "wilderness of rank, useless luxuriance." The narrator speaks of the "hushing up" of the epidemic, which, "despite every denial and concealment ... went on eating its way through the narrow little streets," thereby bringing to the contemporary, ahistorical mind a cluster of unspeakables: insanity, cancer, homosexuality, AIDS. The epidemic is the Other, symbol of all Aschenbach opposes, too shameful to speak of, therefore quashed, silenced. But as with all that is silenced, it ultimately finds horrifying voice—in Aschenbach's case, in the form of a dream:

> It was night, and his senses were alert; for from far off a hubbub was approaching, an uproar, a compendium of noise, a clangor and bell and dull thundering, yells of exultation and a particular howl with a long drawn-out *u* at the end—all of it permeated and dominated by a terrible sweet sound of flute music: by deep-warbling, infamously persistent, shamelessly clinging tones that bewitched the innermost heart. Yet he was aware of a word, an obscure word, but one that gave a name to what was coming: "*the stranger-god!*"... And ... it came tumbling down: a human and animal swarm, a raging rout, flooding the slope with bodies, with flames, with tumult and frenzied dancing ...

[Undated, circa April 1993]

I'm barely passing my courses. School used to be so easy ...

Great was his loathing, great his fear, honorable his effort of will to defend to the last what was his and protect it against the Stranger, against the enemy of the composed and dignified intellect. But the noise, the howling, grew louder, with the echoing cliffs reiterating: it increased beyond measure, swelled up to an enrapturing madness ...

May 13, 1993

I'm reading T.S. Eliot now. In his critical writing he talks about the primacy of impersonality, how all that counts is the text, and how the poet is invisible.

With foaming mouths they raged, they roused each other with lewd gestures and licentious hands, laughing and moaning they thrust the prods into each other's flesh and licked the blood from each other's limbs. But the dreamer now was with them and in them, he belonged to the Stranger-God.

[Undated, circa spring 1993]

"The architect of the universe didn't build a staircase that leads nowhere."
—Grove Patterson

Up the staircase
I plow
And sing
And vanish

They were himself as an orgy of limitless coupling, in homage to the god, began on the trampled, mossy ground. And his very soul savored the lascivious delirium of annihilation.

Annihilation. This orgiastic outflush of words pushes logocentric expression—the mode of Aschenbach and of this particular artwork—to its absolute limits, forcing it to contain such enormity of feeling as to render each word utterly inadequate, helpless. Still, the swirling, feverish striving of this passage does enough to intimate how the rest of the century would unfurl: the two world wars, the sexual revolution, civil rights, women's lib, gay lib, AIDS. And with Aschenbach, garbed gaudily and face painted in a pathetic attempt to impress Tadzio, gazing at the beckoning figure of his shirtless beloved, this novella—one of the most eloquent exegeses on the nature of art ever written—comes to a crashing end with the word "death."

Geist, annihilation.

Vissi d'arte.

(Listen to him, his adoration of this Eurocentric, Global North–privileging, ultimately reactionary, and profoundly homophobic text. What may seem like a harmless Paterian appreciation, a humanistic validation of the universal and timeless, actually contributes to the further diminishment of space for resistance and the ongoing reinforcement of the dominator's culture.)

Thomas Mann (and E.M. Forster) became my model of the queer serious. (Tennessee Williams was a problematic *beau ideal*, given his dissolute life-style and struggles with addiction.) An expansive, subversive mind cloaked in an ascetically genteel persona. An oracle garbed in the beige provisions of the bourgeoisie, dismantling its bathetic constituents with the simple, un-adorned truth. A buttoned-up transmitter of European high culture, nobly sidestepping carnal pleasure for the sake of high art.

But I was practical enough to realize that I couldn't sidestep carnal pleasure forever, that I could only sustain my asceticism until I no longer could. So my full coming-out-to-myself was not precipitated by some epiphanic instant of unbridled physicality but, rather, was an arduous, drawn-out process of intellection. I reminded myself of everything I had read and learned in these ascetic years: that homosexual behaviour is easily observable in the animal kingdom and therefore not "unnatural"; that homosexuality is at least partly genetic and probably nature's way of controlling the human population; that homosexuals were revered in Indigenous cultures around the world; and that many of history's great artists and thinkers—not just Forster and Williams but also, to name a few, Plato, Leonardo, Michelangelo, Wilde, James, Tchaikovsky, Whitman, Lorca, Auden, Genet, Mishima, O'Hara—were homosexuals, able to maintain, to varying degrees, both an impressive artistic output and reasonably active sex lives. (Thomas Mann, by all accounts, repressed most of his homosexual impulses while privately acknowledging them in his diaries.)

I would diligently and incessantly remind myself of these facts whenever self-hate and homophobia set in—a practice that eventually allowed me to call myself "gay" without feeling sick to my stomach. Finally, I declared my sexuality in an essay I wrote for one of my English classes—an event I mark as the beginning of my life as a queer person.

March 21, 1993

What I've learned from Death in Venice:

My body is not safe. I am not meant to engage it.

To do so would be to embrace destruction over creation, the self-annihilating present over the assiduously wrought eternal.

In short, a dishonouring of what art and literature has so clearly revealed: that Nature, in her infinite wisdom, has designed a place for us above the carnal so that we can easier reach the heavens. To stray even slightly would be to fall into the abyss.

There are no better guides for this than Tennessee Williams and Thomas Mann. And with AIDS, Nature has made it apocalyptically clear where she stands.

The epidemic in the novella is the epidemic now afflicting us, the price of unsublimated, improperly channelled desire.

How could Thomas Mann have known so much?

Blanche DuBois and Gustav von Aschenbach. Harrowing artistic embodiments of a hard but ostensibly incontrovertible truth—that only on that staircase can homosexuals thrive and flourish. The opposite is death. Our executioners, as represented by Stanley and Tadzio, idyllic specimens of male pulchritude, are bleak reminders of what happens when queer desire—grandiose, monstrous, overwhelming—abdicates the theoretical for the real. Although I agreed that the tone of the discourse generated by Christian fundamentalists was repugnant, it seemed to me at the time I first read *Death in Venice* that their core message was essentially correct.

June 5, 1993

My birthday today. My present to myself: a project, an experiment, in desensitization.

I rent a porn film tonight. Beautiful, athletic males drilling into one another. Males brimming with the sexy simplicity, the aching purity of single-mindedness. My favourite scene: a hot blond bottom riding an equally hot, darker top, furiously, insanely, unapologetically to orgasm. The world-destroying, category-collapsing madness of sexual defiance.

Immediately afterwards, I watch a television documentary about AIDS. Interviews with young men in the final stages of life. Eyes bulging out of disemboweled, legion-riddled bodies, bulbous channels for the final, overwhelming bursts of life and soul.

Desire and death. The hard, cold reality of risks taken, costs incurred. As a renunciate, as an artist, I stare in the face of both with the insouciant courage of a sociopath.

July 2, 1993

So I came out to my mother today. We were talking about Glenn Gould. She asked me if I thought he was gay. I answered, all geniuses are gay. Then she asked me, "Are you gay?" I said yes. Simple as that.

She didn't seem surprised. She knows I'm a genius.

DOUBLE MELANCHOLY

Am I a modern-day Athena, sprung fully formed from the forehead of Zeus? There is no precedent for intellectual excellence in my family or, for that matter, Filipino culture. We are an unimpressive lot—we've contributed nothing to the world.

So it seems I am an oxymoron: a moral homosexual, a brilliant Filipino. I exist like a self-subverting, self-annihilating Wildean epigram, insidious and invisible, haughtily self-complete.

(The system doesn't even have to try with this brown queer boy. His erasure is a fait accompli.

His obnoxious egomania is societally induced neurosis, a symptom of structural delusion.

As long as the boy is willing, the system will heap care on him as an instrument of its continued legitimation.)

Striving, transcendence, geist. A necessary delusion, perhaps—while in reality I was being invisibilized, I truly believed I was improving myself with my monk-like renunciation of sensuality and fanatical devotion to Western high art. Looking back, I do believe this period was, in the long run, necessary: it gave me the energy to develop my brain, my language, my art—exactly the attributes I needed to survive in a homophobic, white supremacist world.

5 | *CURE:* QUEER AS FOLK

My ascesis ended at age twenty-three. I don't remember any suspense or anxiety leading up to the loss of my virginity, despite my devotion to the ethereal, hardened by AIDS phobia. It transpired, and that was that; as *Sex and the City*'s Carrie Bradshaw remarked after kissing a girl for the first time, "It wasn't bad—kind of like chicken."

T—my first lover—I met in university. He was eight years older, soft-spoken, depression-prone, intellectual. He was kind enough and unthreatening; I had no physical attraction to him whatsoever. A big part of why we went out was because when we first met my mother had started going out with a new man. We were like Debbie Reynolds and Carrie Fisher; I would not be upstaged.

That he was white was not something I consciously dwelled on at the time, but I'm sure my subconscious willed my first lover to be white—not to mention someone with economic privilege and some standing in the particular professional ecology (theatre) I was hell-bent on conquering. These were probably the reasons I stayed with him for two years, despite the flavourless sex and his narcissistic demands that I always put his needs ahead of my own. But his book learning was admirable; on this front I benefited enormously. Even sexually, he was probably the right man for me at the time, as I wasn't ready for the transformation afforded by a truly powerful sexual connection.

Speaking of whiteness, it was during these first years in the professional theatre world—and the queer world—that my race consciousness started to form. Until this point—and even for many years after—I had always identified more strongly as a queer person than as a brown one. In the uber-diverse neighbourhoods where I grew up and went to school, I was ostracized not for being brown but for being queer. But after high school, the spaces I started moving in got whiter and whiter: when I did my creative writing degrees at UBC, only a handful of us majors and graduate students were non-white, and the department had not a single non-white professor. The situation became full-on Norwegian when I started working in professional theatre: nine times out of ten, in my first decade as a professional theatre artist, I was the only non-Caucasian person in the entire room. But even more horrible was that in most of these cases, it was my play that was being workshopped or rehearsed, and the lack of diversity didn't bother me because I'd envisioned the characters as white anyway.

I recall an encounter with a highly esteemed actor. I had been communicating electronically with this artist—admired as one of Canadian theatre's foremost talents—for a number of months, trying to persuade them to act in a workshop of my play. After some convincing, they agreed. When I finally met them in person, a look of utter shock swept over their face.

"Wow," the artist said, "I was expecting a white person."

Too starstruck, and proud that I had secured this Great Artist's services, I said nothing and laughed it off.

May 2, 1999

> Closing night of my play last night. Sold-out house. Dream come true.
>
> Out with the gang for drinks afterwards. P [one of the artists in my play] and I sit next to one another. Being around his vibrations is exhilarating—every part of me feels so intensely, achingly alive.
>
> Later in the night, T joins us. He is depressed and it shows. Everything about him is heavy, colourless, empty of life. I need vibration, light. I need to feel alive.

When I finally broke up with T, it wasn't for the reasons I told him. Like the outwardly defiant but inwardly befuddled Lucy Honeychurch, I lied to myself and others. The truth was, I had fallen madly in love with P and everything he stood for: narcissism, muscles, fast living, hot sex. My previous crushes were childish infatuations compared to what I felt for P: visceral passion for an unrepentant artistic rebel and sexual outlaw.

He worked with me on my second play, which generated city-wide buzz for its depictions of child abuse and graphic simulations of penetrative sex, both straight and queer. It put me on the map, and despite my ego swelling to ever more insufferable heights, I still had the emotional space to feel real gratitude for those who'd brung me. This gratitude only intensified my already intense attraction to P.

He was of average height, body-beautiful, with piercing blue eyes. A weathered old-soul quality elevated his handsomeness beyond the generic. But if his soul was old, his behaviour was adolescent—a reckless partier and avowed sex addict, he was habitually obscenely late for meetings and rehearsals. As the play's producer, I was harangued by the cast to initiate a hard conversation with him about professionalism—a conversation that never happened, because, quite simply, I was smitten. He was gifted, intense, bohemian, iconoclastic; had he come to me and confessed serial rape, I probably would have justified it as part of his creative process.

[Undated, circa May 1999]

> When P tells me he had hot sex last night in Victoria with a Dutch hairstylist—they fucked six times, climaxed each time—my cock springs up like a tent under my briefs. Erotic passion I've known as art, not real life. I'm shocked, perturbed, somewhat jealous, and very envious. Pagan epiphany. Brave new world.

The two months I spent working closely with P remain the most intensely alive period of my life. Everything I did took on purpose and passion—waking up, working out, eating right, looking good—for as clear as day was my life's super-objective: to win the admiration of this living divinity. Even my art, hitherto something I had seen primarily as a means to consolidate my fractured, screaming ego, I started practising just for P. For it was P who held the keys to the realm of beauty—he was both its gatekeeper and its embodiment, the guardian and the thing guarded. He was the radiance that for eight weeks filled the cavity of my life—quite simply, he had cured me of double melancholy.

June 11, 1999

So W [my friend] told me he doesn't think I have a chance with P. After meeting the skinny, nondescript twink P is currently seeing (P assured me it's completely, utterly, absolutely casual, that they're just using each other to get over their respective breakups), he said P is probably only into white guys. I told him to fuck off. I'll probably never speak to him again.

(Besides, he's one to talk—he's a 24-year-old Chinese virgin who's shapeless, nerdy, and whose voice seems to emanate from his nose. As if anyone would ever want him.)

P rejected me. He responded to my declaration of love via email (which struck me as rude, given my love letter to him was handwritten, and I paid fifty-plus dollars to next-day courier it to the town in Alberta where he was shooting a film. Plus, email was still a new thing at the time, with self-declared purists like myself bemoaning it as the death knell of soulful, literate correspondence). He called me beautiful to look at, gifted, an artistic soul-mate, but intimacy with me, he feared, would threaten our creative kinship. I was stunned (I'd maxed out my credit card on psychic hotlines, which all assured me that P would be mine). But, as was my wont in response to deep hurt, I didn't cry, choosing instead to rile myself into action.

I decided that the objective of my life was to be physically splendid. Even my art had to be put to one side until my transformation into an Adonis was complete. I persuaded my mother to invest in a home gym, citing evidence I'd stumbled on that people who worked out at home got better, faster results. In short order, the gym was installed, and so it began: aided by at least $200 of weight-training and diet books, I worked out fiendishly for precisely two hours, five days a week and followed, with unswerving exactitude, Suzanne Somers's regimen for food combining. In two weeks I gained five pounds of muscle and lost ten pounds of fat; I'm a mesomorph, apparently, so gaining muscle is easy. Each workout took on ceremonial fervour, a tortuous guarantor against future heartache. Herculean striving, radical will: I would never be rejected again.

(This is even worse than his blind imbibing of the Western cultural canon—a wholesale internalization, re-inscription, and perpetuation of the most bellicose, violent, and masochistic aspects of white cis gay male hegemony.)

[Undated—circa late summer 1999]

bloom

blandishment

bosch

Triceps presses, biceps curls, cable glute kickbacks, lateral pull-downs, butterfly presses, shoulder shrug supersets. Triceps before biceps, full body not split, three weeks on, one off, cardio after weights. Absolutely no refined sugar, eat nothing after seven p.m.; to breach the program was to succumb to mediocrity, nausea, the muck.

Within a couple of months, I started to consistently receive compliments on my body. I wrote each and every compliment down in my notebook, as reassurance that fulfillment of Apolline invulnerability was nigh.

After approximately four months of working out, I deemed myself present-able enough to start placing ads on phone lines (online dating sites had yet to achieve world domination). My ads were unadorned and, at least to my mind, completely transparent: "Five foot eight, athletic build, black hair, brown eyes. Looking for casual hook-ups, maybe more." (I'd re-record my ad multiple times until I was at least semi-convinced that the timbre of my voice was sufficiently butch.) So I'd meet with guys, sight unseen, and although I ended up in bed with a few (just blow jobs for the longest while; I wasn't ready to go the whole nine yards), most were one-time coffee dates (with a few saying goodbye—not always graciously—within two minutes of meeting). There was one date who said he'd call me back but never did; when I revisited his profile on the phone line two days later, I noticed he'd changed his ad to say "white men only."

Suddenly, the reason behind the puzzled looks on the faces of a lot of the men I met—all white—became clear. I didn't mention my race in my ad because I didn't think it mattered; begrudgingly, I added "Spanish-Filipino" to my ad, and specified that I was looking to meet only Caucasian men.

(As Karen Walker of Will & Grace *might say, "Honey, do you know how many things are wrong with that paragraph?"*

First, let's problematize the hierarchization of sex acts, implicit in the euphemizing of anal intercourse as "the whole nine yards" against the diminution of fellatio with the word "just." But this is "just" foreshadowing of the wholesale inscription of hierarchy to come: namely, the perpetuation of white supremacy in his dating life, as evidenced by his outing himself as "Spanish-Filipino"—the "Spanish" strategically placed as a modifier—read: skin whitener—despite the fact that probably no more than one-sixteenth of his ancestry is Spanish. Indeed, this is common practice among Filipinxs, easily one of the most colonized, self-hating peoples on earth: the usually exaggerated and often false claims to European ancestry.

As for his preference for white men—this is, sadly, all too common among queer men of colour. But who can blame them when virtually all the models of desirability in the queer male world [whether twink, bear, muscleboy, leather, BDSM, etc.] are white? It's insufficient to call a preference "just a preference"— neuroscience has shown that preferences are malleable and profoundly shaped by our social environments. So it's hardly rocket science that white supremacy leads to the widespread preference for white sexual partners.)

It was during this period that I encountered advertisements for an exclusive screening of a British miniseries called *Queer as Folk* at the local cinematheque. Apparently, in its native land it had elicited both praise and outrage for its graphically frank treatment of queer life, in particular its depiction of the anal deflowering of a fifteen-year-old boy. I read the synopsis in the cinematheque's superbly written monthly guide (it remains to this day one of the best arts publications in the city). Ordinarily, I would have deemed a television series beneath me, but at this point, high culture no longer held me in thrall—my new priority was to earn entry into the foyer of fuckables, and *Queer as Folk*, with its promise of no-holds-barred Uranian fornicating, seemed made to order. (And I was comforted by the fact that its Britishness would spare me wholesale condemnation from the literati.)

The atmosphere in the cinematheque was electric. The event began with a stirring, impassioned speech by the organizer about the cardinal importance of queer images and the community's access to them. (Context: Vancouver was the site of a landmark court battle that went all the way to the Supreme Court about the LGBTQ bookstore Little Sister's decade-long tussle with Canada Customs over the seizure of books and artwork under the country's obscenity laws.) I remember the actual visual experience of watching the show as being less than ideal—the picture was at times grainy, but more significantly, it was *physically* a TV series—with its diminished aspect ratio—on a cinematic big screen. But these flaws actually had the effect of intensifying the experience: it felt like the audience was in on something bootlegged, sub rosa.

[Undated—circa late fall 2000]

[Detailed notes on Queer as Folk, *upon ordering and watching the just-released video straight from the UK, which allowed me to practise deep-structure analysis of it.]*

• *Theme song—entirely in a major key and therefore wholly, utterly joyous, not a hint of any of the darkness we have come to expect from gay-themed plays and films. The xylophone is prominent, as are drums and jungle voices. The sidelining of Apollo, the centring of Dionysus.*

• *1st exterior shot tracks men filing out of Babylon nightclub onto Canal Street, the show's geographical and metaphorical epicentre (the physical connotations of the word "canal" and its containment of the word "anal" creating a doubling effect that may simultaneously italicize and cancel out). It's as major a character in the story as Stuart, Vince, or Nathan, where men instigate copulations or simply run into each other again and again.*

• *Stuart on the prowl. As he slithers down Canal Street, "I Feel Good Things for You" by Daddy's Favourite (actually a club mix of the original Patrice Rushen song "Haven't You Heard") plays in the background—icy, metallic, unsparingly direct, and doggedly insistent. The repeated tonic-to-flat-seventh cadence that weaves the song together is the sonic expression of the eternal question that governs gay male life: "Do you want to fuck? Do you want to fuck?" When Aidan Gillen's Stuart Jones asks the question, the answer, one would imagine, is usually affirmative. Gillen is not conventionally handsome, which makes his casting a stroke of genius: what QAF italicizes is authenticity, not glamour.*

• Indeed, all of QAF is a radical deconstructive project. First, its repudiation of the morose AIDS narratives we've come to expect from anything billed as "gay-themed." AIDS is brought up only twice in the entire series—in one instance it's unapologetically appropriative, in the form of a red ribbon Stuart pins on at work to signal his predilections to a closeted associate, whom he ultimately shags. Second, as mentioned, its privileging of authenticity over glamour. None of the men in the series are impossibly beautiful, which makes the show both more accessible and, abjuring sterile high glamour, rawly energetic. The biggest nostrum punctured, however, is one that extends beyond gaydom, but whose puncturing in a gay context puts gaydom at risk of wholesale vilification: the pristineness of child sexuality. Stuart fucking fifteen-year-old Nathan in episode 1 makes it writ large that there will be no kowtowing to demands to keep it respectable. QAF is an unbroken gesture of unadulterated defiance.

"That's it. Slowly. That's all of them. All the football team. All of them naked and in shorts. And the referee is going, 'Yes, yes, yes.' In we go." So says Stuart as he enters Nathan's posterior orifice. The reference to football, the image of an entire football team filling his cavity, the refreshing masculinity of the two lovers (neither exhibit any stereotypically gay mannerisms)—QAF portrays gayness as an unabashedly masculine phenomenon, a glorious embodiment of Camille Paglia's take on male homosexuality as a heroic act, the ultimate flight from the tyrannical triumvirate of Woman/Mother/Mother Nature.

• The actors break the fourth wall on four occasions in episode 1 (Vince and Stuart each have one monologue, Nathan two). If the masculinity of these three gay characters is atypical, these unmistakably theatrical insertions circle us back to what is typically gay: theatre has historically played a formative role in gay male

identity. These monologues pay homage to that fact, but it's worth noting that this wall-breaking only occurs in episode 1; the rest of the series is cinematic, seamlessly committed to naturalistic illusionism—a gay colonizing of a more mainstream, popular, and, consequently, typically more homophobic medium.

• Throughout the show, the camera movement is elegant, expansive, and expansionist.* When Nathan returns to Canal Street after his night with Stuart, the camera slowly pans from his trepidatious arrival at the bar to the trio of Stuart, Vince, and Phil, capturing men and drag queens dancing to Divine's "You Think You're a Man" in a phantasmagoric visual wash of black, red, blue, and green. The pan to Stuart, Vince, and Phil is indescribably hip—this threesome of good-looking, well-dressed, masculine men smoking, drinking, and chatting with cool confidence presents a striking new image of gay men—one that offers straights an alternative paradigm for thinking of gays, and offers gays necessary uplift, a means for self-assertion.

• Vince. The sensitive, vulnerable, non-threatening third of the gay male personality, the main parts of which are represented by QAF's three main characters. Though he's arguably more attractive physically than Stuart, he lacks the latter's swagger and thus ability to bed men—whether they admit to it or not, Vince is the character most gay men relate to: lovelorn, vaguely yearning for a level of approval that is forever elusive.

* And when I say "expansionist" I mean colonizing, or, more precisely, reverse-colonizing: these bold, unapologetic images take up space where they have historically been repudiated.

(• "Expansionism"—or, more precisely, "counter-expansionism," may indeed be a necessary means of levelling the playing field, but it's worth considering if an approach that privileges authenticity, that protects the integrity—and survival—of marginal locations would not in the end be more transformative.

• Voice Proper's conceptual framework vis-à-vis sexual identities is based on an oh-so-quaint rigid gay-straight binary—convenient as a starting point, and reflective of where mainstream discourse was at the turn of the last century—but démodé and simplistic, and ultimately colonial/colonizing and destructive.

• *The idea that* QAF *presents entirely new or alternative paradigms must be challenged. That queer men—or, more accurately in the context of* QAF, *gay cis white men—have typically been seen by the dominant culture as promiscuous, drug-ingesting, all-night partiers is standard knowledge to the point of being a truism. The point that it presents an "alternative" to AIDS-focused, defeatist narratives is well taken, but in the bigger picture what it covers is familiar, even hoary territory: promiscuity, licentiousness, and cis-white-able-bodied-male-centricism.*

• *We've firmly established the narrator's misogyny, and now we see it informing how he hierarchizes queer men. Effeminacy as stain, embarrassment to manhood: what is extolled is the strutting masculinity that traumatized his youth. Queer men exalting precisely what oppresses them is part of the larger suite of masochistic poses [women lionizing men, Indigenous and racialized folks giving credence to white supremacy] that naturalizes the status quo.*

• *Fifteen-year-old Nathan's deflowering by Stuart is statutory rape. That* QAF *never interrogates this power imbalance is itself a re-inscription of the status quo, where Nathan's real pain at being treated like a one-off shag is dismissed as mere youthful naïveté.*

• *The narrator's view of* QAF *as a revolutionary enterprise is laughable, given how this show—both the original British version and especially its North American retread—re-inscribes the status quo on the profoundest structural level. Capitalizing on the hunger of its historically marginalized queer viewership to be full participants in "the game," it creates in this demographic a need to merge with pop culture products that reflect them—hence,* QAF *mugs, T-shirts, posters, smartphone cases, stickers. As the critical theorist Theodor Adorno argued, we are as programmed, conditioned, tyrannized—unfree—at play as we are at work.)*

January 16, 2001

> In the sketchy old bathhouse in New Westminster. One guy in my mouth, the other in my ass. For a minute it feels like rape, but I hunker down and soldier on. Upon ejaculation they leave, no pillow talk, nary a thank you.

(More later about the analogy to rape.)

CURE: QUEER AS FOLK

[*Undated—circa late fall 2000*]

[*Notes on* QAF *continued*]

• *The show's token effeminate, Alexander—incredibly annoying, he sports a brand of physical unattractiveness that is quintessentially British: pasty and horsey, with misaligned teeth. But he provides the show with some of its biggest laughs, and the function he serves is ultimately crucial: stereotypical effeminacy as object of ridicule, laughed at by other gays as much as heterosexuals, thereby isolating and denormalizing it.*

• *More instances of the panning, expansive camera mentioned earlier. First, the magical moment when Nathan and Donna enter Babylon for the first time. The camera pulls away as they disappear into the dance floor and the shot swells into a panorama of sinewy half-lit bodies dancing to "I Feel Good Things for You." The* mise en scène *is stunning, made unforgettable by the undulating figure of the shirtless male on the platform. The camera is calm, gentle, unassuming, letting us explore for ourselves this brave new world. Nothing else I have seen on film or television has more perfectly captured the wonder—the awesomeness—of subcultural discovery than this unedited, singularly graceful shot.*

• *Second, Stuart's threesome with the two Adonises he picks up at Babylon. The camera pans from a generic, quotidian object (a telephone) to something divinely transgressive (the writhing, sweaty bodies of Stuart and his two Adonises). Adding to the subversiveness is the presence of Stuart's camera, which we see filming the sordid proceedings. The texturedness of this short scene is astonishing. First, the visual crescendo from the telephone to the orgy signals the ravishing, all-encompassing, all-consuming power of sex, under which all else must buckle and surrender. Second, the scene's show-within-a-show aspect cuts two ways—on one hand, reinforcing sexuality's vibrant performativity; on the other, doubling this performativity and paradoxically cancelling it out, thereby foregrounding its primal, chthonic naturalness.*

• *But even more magical is the earlier scene in Babylon where Stuart secures said threesome. To fully grasp why Stuart's success here is so meaningful to gay viewers, one must understand the deep need this scene addresses. The astonishment, admiration, and envy with which the rest of the gang watches Stuart ensnare the pulchritudinous pair is the astonishment, admiration, and envy of the whole of gaydom. For to land a man is to make us forget—temporarily, at least—our history of being bullied and rejected by other men. Each time we score, we assuage the pain, and are reconciled, at least for a time, with both other men and our own manhood. At the end of the scene, to the dying beats of the electrifying Builds Like a Skyscraper mix of the OT Quartet's "Hold That Sucker Down," the camera pans up and out to the white ether: cure attained, transcendence achieved.*

• The death of Phil—the one truly dark moment in the series. That he doesn't die of AIDS is testament, once again, to the show's shunning of maudlin, mawkish narratives. To die a drug-related death is at least to die of an assertive act, borne of a conscious choice to expand one's experience. Again, borrowing from Paglia, this is an exercise in freedom, defying the respectable, and therefore heroic.

• A word about Nathan: he is annoying as fuck.

(• To say the least, it's telling that Voice Proper made no notes about the racism in the show, which is so extreme and obvious that one might mistake it for parody. Alexander jets in with his Japanese lover, Li, who speaks no English and, it is revealed, is a hooker who's only with Alexander because the latter owes him money. The problems start right off the top with the character's name, which is actually Chinese—an all-too-predictable Orientalist blanketing-over of specificity and difference. But with each appearance or mention of this unfortunate character, the show simply digs itself a deeper and deeper hole—prostitution, money-grubbing, and, finally, most tragic of all, Vince's nickname for him: "Fu Manchu." That this line was assigned to the show's most sympathetic character is proof that the show's creators deemed the line totally harmless, indicative of the white supremacy undergirding the show. Of its nineteen speaking characters, only two, besides Li, are people of colour, both merely accessories or obstacles for the white characters. The character of Donna is likeable enough, but she is little more than Nathan's sidekick, and although she delivers one of the show's most memorable lines—at Nathan's charge that because she's straight she's part of the "fascist heterosexist orthodoxy," she snaps, "I'm black. And I'm a girl. Try that for a week."—it feels like an afterthought, white-liberal first aid rather than radical surgery. Voice Proper is brown and queer, and QAF invisibilizes him; that he cites this show as fundamental to his sexual awakening is problematic, given how it erases his existence while ostensibly confirming it. He is neither beautiful nor desirable, according to the dictates of QAF's world, but once the coloured lights start flashing, it's blinding spectacle—white ether indeed.

• Voice Proper's focus on sex—or, more accurately, the mode of his focus—has the effect of romanticizing and, consequently, essentializing it. He re-inscribes the notion of sex as something unquestioned and absolute, a primal force that pre-exists us and over which we have no agency, thereby denying the numerous ways in which it is a performative gesture in a specific context, conditioned by a particular discourse. He ignores the infinite possibilities of both sex and human agency; what is erased is multiplicity, nuance, difference.

• Once again betraying extreme femmephobia, the narrator is exceedingly harsh on Alexander. The swipe at his Britishness, though, demonstrates backbone and self-esteem.

• Although the passage about Stuart's sexual triumph in Babylon is moving, we must problematize how it deploys a semantics of pain, which equates queerness with rupture from some essential, prelapsarian state.

• Voice Proper has cited Camille Paglia several times now in this book. Like that earlier paleo-individualistic pseudo-philosopher Ayn Rand, she's a pin-up for adrift young brainiacs looking for simplistic templates for ostentatious intellectualizing.

• Voice Proper has used rape as metaphor several times in this book. It wouldn't be naive to assume that he has been sexually assaulted—but he has not. Artistic expression is not above scrutiny: we must interrogate this display of entitlement.

• Voice Proper's stance towards HIV/AIDS has moved from fear and loathing to facile dismissal. There is healing to be had; it will require a generous and unlimited embrace. AIDS, as it connotes obliteration, is the final frontier. For the narrator to embrace obliteration is to embrace de(con)struction of every value he has ever extolled.)

DOUBLE MELANCHOLY

March 24, 2001

QAF = the lubricant that facilitates my entry into the nightclub world. Somehow, I've been more reticent to explore nightclubs than bathhouses—probably because it has a strong collectivist aspect, while bathhouses are more feline: it's all about seeing and conquering. But QAF has made nightclubs too picturesque to ignore.

I went to the Odyssey last night. Not as picturesque as Babylon, but I'll take it. About an hour in I spot P and his boyfriend on the dance floor. Later, I see him dancing on the platform, shirtless.

P dancing shirtless on the Odyssey platform—a visual image I infuse with intention. Mercurially, violently beautiful. I will be that one day.

And one day, like Stuart with Vince, he'll realize he made a mistake with me. But by that time I won't care, I'll be so out of his league.

May 16, 2001

Pounding me
Pounding my ass the way they do in porn
I'm living the dream
Coz this is as good as I dreamt it would be
His touch   his smell   his technique
HIM
He takes me out of me
Makes me forget about me
I know I'm getting close
His pounding accelerates
He arches his back
He gasps the gasp
Like clockwork he pulls out
Pecks me on the lips
Gets up   showers   pats me on the head   leaves

Before my coloured lights
Always before my coloured lights

[Undated, circa late spring 2001]

The weather's warming up, warm enough to wear tank tops. My biceps and triceps I now share with the world. Yesterday I notice two girls on the bus check me out.

Last night, I go to the Odyssey. An exhilarating remix of the Ultra Naté song "Found a Cure" starts playing and easily, organically, I ascend the platform and start dancing. There's no epiphany, no self-coercion—the time has simply come. I've become what I wanted to be, something that bruises, torments, kills.

[Undated, circa late summer 2001]

In Fredericton and frisky. Three guys in 48 hours. The first, and the best of them, is a hot Acadian with a killer smile. I ride him senseless, he comes inside me. He fucks me again, doggie style, then comes all over my face. When I awake this morning I'm still horny—I want to come with a guy before I leave—so I hook up with another bloke I meet online. He's nowhere near as hot as the Acadian but whatever, he's meat. I don't come, so when he's gone I go online and invite over another guy—he has swarthy good looks and is an aggressive fucker. He bends me over, drills me and finishes in three minutes. He slaps my ass when he leaves, tells me I'm his first Asian, that I'm hot as hell and I've made him crave more Asian ass, and it's too bad there are so few of us in Atlantic Canada, much less Freddy, that he never thought he'd be into Asians and wants to thank me for "expanding his palate."

I know I should love myself, but I don't. I don't love myself. Until I do, I might as well have lots of fun along the way.

The bullheaded, unwavering, unremitting intensity I habitually poured into my work spilled over, naturally, into my sex life. I would not tolerate imperfection; I refused to admit defeat. Every snub, every rejection—whether real or imagined—was met with unbridled, apoplectic fury.

Case in point: this handsome, muscular triathlete I hooked up with once. After an unbelievably hot encounter in that shady old bathhouse in New West, I asked him if he wanted to hook up again when he was back in town (he lived up north). He said yes. As I usually did in convos of that sort, I took him at his word.

About a year later, I saw him online and his profile said he was in Vancouver. I messaged him to inquire if he wanted to meet; he said yes.

We met in a bar in the Village. We talked for about an hour—it was brighter there than it was in the bathhouse—and it struck me that his face wasn't as attractive as I remembered. But it didn't matter—he had a hot body and a deep, masculine voice. And I hadn't been shagged in a while, so I was single-minded about getting laid.

Abruptly, casually, he said he was meeting friends in about an hour. I was puzzled. "So we're not having sex tonight?"

"Probably not." He excused himself to use the restroom.

I was numb. He might as well have waxed off all my body hair in one fell pull.

As soon as he came back, language returned to me. "I thought we were meeting for sex."

He said no, he wasn't free tonight.

"So when *are* you free?"

He wasn't sure; he'd get back to me. He apologized for the misunderstanding, shook my hand, then left.

I could've bought that it was a genuine misunderstanding, that he really did have friends he was meeting that night. But I didn't buy it because all I cared about was the only truth that mattered: that I was disgusting, repulsive, that this sexy triathlete I thought fucked me never actually fucked me, that I made it up in my head because I was narcissistic and delusional, for how could a sexy triathlete possibly find me attractive? I had no inkling of what was real anymore—all I knew was that the exquisite skin I had so assiduously constructed had been ripped off me, and that underneath it was not bones but a vacuum.

So, for my sanity, to feel real again, I chose acrimony, war. Not long after we parted, I start texting him every hour, asking him in about twenty-three different ways why he made me meet him under false pretenses. Eventually, the texts diminished to mere question marks, while accelerating in frequency to two to three an hour. I switched tactics, told him I forgave him, that I wanted to see him again before he left town. His non-response simply emboldened me: I would not rest until I got my due.

I continued to text him. He blocked me online, so I created a new, fake profile from which to harangue him. I started calling him from a blocked number; each time he picked up, I hung up. Finally, when he picked up I played an audiotape of me having an orgasm, cued to the precise point where my top fucked me to climax.

At last, he left me a voice message. "Listen, buddy, why don't you stop acting so freaking immature? I don't get the point of it, I really don't, and it just proves that you're as big a loser as I thought you were."

Mission accomplished. I got my due.

March 29, 2004

Had a foursome with a white guy and two Surrey Sikh closet cases at the F212 in the Village last night. They're Punjabi, they tell us, it's not accepted in their culture. It's like, tell me something I don't know, I wasn't born yesterday. They're my first East Indians, and hopefully not my last. The hotter of the two of them fucked me without mercy, as if plundering the gutter in pursuit of the stars.

The first time I came with a guy (and it took a while—partly because I had trouble getting out of my head, and partly because most of the guys I was with only cared about *their* orgasms) was at a swanky hotel downtown. He was handsome, Jewish, Floridian, older—actually, significantly older than what his online ad said; after we hooked up, I Googled him and discovered that he was my mother's age. But he had a youthful, masculine energy and a decent, solid body, a sexy East Coast accent, and a glowing Florida tan.

We met in the hotel lobby; I perked up as soon as I saw him. Whether it was pheromones or kismet, we were at each other's mercy. In the elevator he said

I was gorgeous, even more beautiful than in my pictures. He said the magic words; he sealed the evening's fate.

THE FOUR PHASES OF SEEING ONESELF:

1. Locked lips as soon as we got to his room. Ordered up drinks—gin on the rocks for him, wine for me. Talked about Vancouver ("my first time here—it's gorgeous"), George W. Bush ("hate him"), work (he's a lawyer), Israel/Palestine ("I'm Jewish *and* pro-Palestinian"). Told me he screwed another fella last night, so on that front, so far, Vancouver had been good to him. Ran his finger up and down my arm and under my shirt, all the while telling me how sexy I am. Partly the wine but mostly the words: I was relaxed and turned on because *I was seeing myself.* Usually, sex was about the letting-go of self—but in my case I had no self to let go of. But now this quality guy was making me see *me*. We made out, lustily; we moved to the bed.

2. Fucking me on the edge of the bed, my legs arched over his shoulders. He stopped, kissed me, and without pulling out, lifted me up, carried me to the bathroom, set me down on the sink, and started thrusting again. Behind me was a mirror with flaps; he pulled one out so we had a view. I turned to it and saw a little more of me; he was fucking me into existence.

3. I was on top of him, riding his cock, glistening with sweat and lube and baby oil. *Yes, that's it,* I was seeing all of me now, every bit of me all at once. And hearing and feeling and smelling and tasting. This must be what it's like in heaven, where you can hear flowers and taste music. *Yes, that was all of me, each and every part of me*, the parts I hated became the parts I loved, because they confirmed that I exist. *That's it, that's all of me, warts and all, every part of me*, I grabbed his chest as if for dear life as he stroked my cock to orgasm.

4. As I got dressed, he told me I was hotter than the guy he had last night. I hugged him, pecked him on the lips, winked at him, departed.

[Undated—circa late fall 2000]

[Notes on QAF *continued]*

Stuart and Vince. The greatest gay love story yet. The hot oaf and the sensitive enabler, the latter enduring the former's innumerable peccadillos and, in the process, revealing—and winning—the former's heart. The unfolding of their relationship is exquisite—the fast but painful flashes of Vince's sexual jealousy, the quick but touching glimpses of Stuart's love for Vince.

The most beautiful love scene in gay TV or film has little sexual about it: when Stuart and Vince break their estrangement and meet at a café, and Vince expresses disbelief that his rich and successful boyfriend is so in love with him, Stuart replies, "You go to work, you go for a drink, you sit and watch cheap science fiction. Small and tiny world. What is there that is so impressive about that? What is there to love? ... It was good enough for me."

And the final scene is extraordinary: with Tatjana's bittersweet "Santa Maria" playing behind him, a morose Stuart, having relinquished Vince, is on the prowl again in Babylon, and about to hook up with the hot druggie responsible for Phil's death (none of the characters know this, of course, because the druggie fled the scene). But Vince, after ending it with his boyfriend, arrives just in time to break it up by beckoning to Stuart from the dance floor to join him on the platform. After chuckling and refusing twice, Stuart accepts the invite, and the show ends with the friends/lovers dancing into the night.

(That QAF *ultimately extols the relationship of Stuart and Vince is proof of how misguided Voice Proper is in his adoration of this show. If, as the show's ending suggests, Stuart and Vince do end up together, it's clear that sex is not the defining aspect of their relationship, as hinted at by one of the songs played in the final scene, "Deeper Love." So, ultimately, by privileging the "soul-bond" of Stuart and Vince over Stuart's primarily sexual relationship with Nathan and his numerous one-night stands,* QAF *hierarchizes, desexualizes, and homonormalizes queer relationships.)*

October 2, 2004

I had coffee with the porn producer yesterday. Young Filipino guy, actually pretty hot. He thanks me for answering the ad, says they're really eager to start doing gay stuff. He says I'm what they're looking for—good-looking, in shape, and that not being white is a bonus (I guess even "the industry" has diversity quotas). He makes it clear he's not gay (Filipino machismo), but that he's confident I'll work out. He makes an appointment for me to meet the gay guy who heads up their "gay branch."

The appointment was for this morning. I get as far as the elevator and actually step out of it when it arrives at the designated floor, but in six seconds I'm back inside it, pressing the "down" button. Can't do it.

August 17, 2005

[An email sent to me by a trick in response to a tome-length email I sent him in which I attacked him for not fucking me after I travelled twelve hours by bus to his home in the Kootenays.]

From: F_M

To: Chris Gatchalian

Subject: [No subject]

For a writer, you sure are long-winded. Aren't writers encouraged to express themselves succinctly?

You have no substance, which explains your craving to be filled.

May 24, 2006

Haven't been sleeping well lately. Slept only a few hours last night because I was burning with rage about not being nominated for a Jessie [Vancouver's annual professional theatre awards]. Obviously I'm a fucking failure, a worthless piece of trash; either that or people hate me, or are crazy-jealous, or whatever.

M better produce my fucking play if she knows what's good for her. It's been my life's work the last two years; it will not be for naught. If I can't make it as a writer there's no point in anything. Writing is all I can or want to do, I'm good for nothing else.

Also kinda nervous about these two guys I'm meeting tonight. They text me last night asking if I'd be up to taking both of their dicks in my ass at once. I say sure, but what else can I say? They're both over 8 inches and I need something to make me matter, and if being a receptacle for a couple of horsedicks is all I'm good for right now, so be it.

Shortly after the date of this last journal entry, I had my breakdown. I was put on anti-anxiety meds and two different sedatives. To top it off, I had to confront a long-standing fear: although I always used protection during sex, there were the theoretical possibilities of infection—an unknown tear in a condom, an abrasion in the mouth, saliva that wouldn't quite kill the virus upon contact—that, as was my wont, triggered weekly calls for reassurance to AIDS hotlines. Two negative tests at, respectively, the one-month and three-month marks did little to quell my fears, for I was convinced that I would be one of the especial few that wouldn't test positive until the six-month mark. So it was a half year of self-imposed retreat from the world, from the earthly pleasures I indulged in but never felt at home with. Everything closed in on me—every fear I entertained regarding meaning and nothingness, danger and death. But with this came also a circling back, a return, to what I *did* feel at home with, to what had always been there to catch me.

October 7, 2006

Emily Dickinson, Gerard Manley Hopkins, T.S. Eliot, Virginia Woolf.

I haven't been out the last three days. I have everything I need right here.

Each of their words is a step outside of myself, to what is purer, larger, more embracing.

For the first time in months, I see the sky.

(*Touching, Voice Proper's salvation through art. Too bad all it promotes is inertia.*)

Afflicted with double melancholy, I obsessively pursued the most intense cure available: sex. Transcendence, happiness, nirvana, God—aren't these simply different names for what is essentially one thing: the feeling of no longer needing anything, of being, in effect, cured? It may be tragically temporary, but it doesn't make it less sublime.

Art offers a cure that is more reliable and enduring, so it is once again the centre of my life.

6 | BESOTTED: CAMILLE PAGLIA & SUSAN SONTAG

After the six-month test confirmed I was HIV-negative, I felt mentally and emotionally fit enough to play the field again, in moderation.

After some one-night stands and casual flings, I met X, a young professor originally from Athens, now based in New York. Yes, we hooked up, but it was more than that. He changed my life.

Prior to meeting him, both my professional and personal lives revolved around furious striving and blind ambition, qualities I saw embodied in both the work and personae of the two artistically besotted women who served as my early intellectual role models: Camille Paglia and Susan Sontag. A helped me relax and settle somewhat into the here and now, and started me on the tortuous journey towards being that most frightening of things: myself.

Ever since I can remember, I was told I was smart. Growing up, this gave me enough confidence to withstand the taunts hurled at me for being shy, hypersensitive, socially awkward, unathletic. Fortunately for me, our society (ostensibly) places a high premium on intellectual intelligence, so on that front, at least, I had an advantage.

(To a certain extent, anyway: I was what memoirist and social critic Richard Rodriguez calls a "scholarship boy," adept at memorizing and regurgitating "facts," not so adept at interrogating and challenging them. Not because I actually attempted it and realized I wasn't good at it, but simply because it never occurred to me that it was, or could be, an option. All that mattered to me in school was to be "the best," period.)

So, from the beginning, I knew I'd be something brainy when I grew up. Sadly, mainstream culture doesn't provide nerds with many public role models—for all the lip service our society pays to intellectual acumen, its pop culture arm is decidedly anti-intellectual. (At least in North America: in the States, ostensible devotion to democratic ideals precludes appreciation for anything deemed hoity-toity; in Canada, unapologetic intelligence is anathema to our credo of modesty.)

So when I discovered Camille Paglia, I felt as though my vague intellectual aspirations had found tangible human form. The first openly queer contemporary thinker I came across, she was an unabashed worshipper of Western high art: she sported encyclopedic, omnivorous knowledge of world history and culture; she was brash, arrogant, pugnacious, and confident. (Yes, she had an annoying voice and spoke a thousand words a minute, but she exhibited an almost absolute self-certainty—a certainty that gave me much-needed comfort at the time.) Although my current opinion of Paglia is one of only partial admiration, my first encounters with her were akin to a godless but spiritually hungry child meeting a prophet.

In short, I was besotted.

I stumbled upon her work when I was seventeen and first coming out to myself, a struggle exacerbated by the fact that at the time gay rights (the term "LGBTQ" had not yet gained currency) was a lightning rod for controversy everywhere. In Canada, legislation in the House of Commons to protect queers from workplace discrimination was brought to a screeching halt, thanks to acrimonious debate and divisions in every party. South of the border, the situation was even more volatile: while the Democratic Party's presidential candidate, Bill Clinton, was courting the queer vote by promising, if elected, to lift the ban on queers in the military, the GOP had declared war on us, with Pat Buchanan calling us "sodomites" for whom "AIDS is nature's retribution." A ballot measure in Oregon that would have enshrined homosexuality as "abnormal, wrong, unnatural and perverse" in the state constitution failed, but in Colorado, an initiative to ban municipalities from passing ordinances protecting queers from discrimination was approved, leading to calls from Barbra Streisand and other luminaries to boycott the state. The common theme I deduced was that I was a mutant, an unwelcome disruption to the system, an impediment to things unfolding as they were meant to. I was the subject of either hatred and ridicule by those opposed to my existence, or compassion and charity by ostensible supporters.

Certainly, Paglia made no attempt to normalize who I was. "Homosexuality is not 'normal,'" she says outright in her essay collection *Vamps & Tramps*. What she did, though, through an act of Nietzschean transvaluation, was help me to see non-normativity in a different light. "[Homosexuality] is a challenge to the norm," she continues, "hence its eternally revolutionary character."

In her 1990 article in *Esquire* called "Homosexuality at the Fin de Siècle" she mentions "two principal kinds of male homosexuality," the first being female-identified and linked to drag queens, and the second hypermasculine, representing "a turning away from the mother and a heroic rebellion against her omnipotence." Paglia argues that "there is nothing deviant or effeminate in this kind of homosexuality. On the contrary, I view the modern gay male as occupying the ultimate point on a track of intensifying masculinity shooting away from the mother, who begins every life story."

She goes on to observe that "men, driven by sexual anxiety away from their mothers, [form] group alliances by male bonding to create the complex structures of society, art, science and technology." She credits male homosexuality for "pushing outward into risky, alien territory" and for being "progressive and, overall, intellectually stimulating." She ends the essay by praising queer male promiscuity, calling queer men "guardians of the masculine impulse. To have anonymous sex in a dark alleyway is to pay homage to the dream of male freedom."

Looking back, as a male, I don't think I've ever genuinely felt unfree (though I certainly did as a *queer* male—but that's not what Paglia is speaking of here). But at the time it didn't matter; I was besotted by her romantic worship of masculinity, a quality that always struck me as exotic and never something I truly possessed. It was also the first time I had heard or read anyone describe queerness as something positive and active, as an embodiment of moral agency. Yes, old-fashioned misogyny informed her thinking, but for a seventeen-year-old queer boy desperate to find justification for his existence, that hardly mattered. My intellectual hunger was satiated as well by her learned references to both high and low culture, and her contextualizing of the topic of homosexuality in broad historical terms. And, yes, her mother-theory made sense to me, given my own powerful mother and my wish at seventeen to escape her shadow.

For all these reasons, this short, extremely problematic essay—besides being misogynistic, it resorts to clichéd swipes at lesbian sex as being boring and "inert," and is grounded in long-disproven Freudian gender theories—remains one of the most personally galvanizing and empowering pieces of writing I've ever read. Jazzed, I went to the bookstore to purchase her infamous tome *Sexual Personae: Art and Decadence from Nefertiti to Emily Dickinson.*

(Once in a while, to justify its homophobia and misogyny, the system has to produce someone like Paglia, a person who identifies as being from a marginalized background—in this case, a queer, genderfluid woman—yet who claims that queer folks actually should be marginalized, and women actually deserve to be raped. The right wouldn't be nearly as strong as it is if didn't have at least a few Uncle Toms, Aunt Jemimas, and Auncle Jemimatoms waving its flag.

One can only imagine the true extent of Paglia's self-hatred, and the immense high she gets when she receives approval from the far right.)

August 6, 2007

> *X left today. I'm in shock that someone like X—with his swagger, his Greekness, his worldliness, his sophistication, would want someone like me ...*
>
> *I suppose I should feel flattered, self-satisfied, proud. But all I feel is that he's left a hole inside me that may never be filled again.*
>
> *He says he'll email me when he gets home, and that I can call him whenever I want. The school of hard knocks has taught me to take everything every trick says with a grain of salt. I'll just savour the smell of him on me, and be grateful I had him.*

Since I didn't have a religious upbringing, what the Bible provides for others, *Sexual Personae* provided, and still provides, for me: I am still recovering from and defining myself against it. Its pithy, biting pronouncements ring with the unalloyed certainty of an oracle; every line in every one of its nearly seven hundred pages seared my brain like the melismatic stylings of a great gospel singer. I was a spiritually adrift, sexually questioning, culturally displaced Generation X teenager—a white-on-the-inside brown queer dude, with no mind whatsoever to call his own. I was desperate for diamond-hard absolutes about the world, and *Sexual Personae* handed me them, word for scintillating word.

I still maintain it's a stunning book—compulsively readable, eccentrically untrendy, grandly operatic. But, beautiful as the writing is, its range is exceedingly small. Its basic thesis—that nature is malevolent and biology is destiny—is but one of innumerable possible takes on the human condition. (And a mundane one at that: too often what we write off as "natural" is what we are unwilling or too lazy to change. These days, I'm much more invested in human progress and transformation.) The entire book unfolds on a playing field in which there are only ever two competitors: Art/Science/Technology/Law/Society/Apollo/Order on one side, and Nature/the Chthonic/Ooze/Muck/Dionysus/Chaos on the other—with the latter always winning in the end. The respite art offers from nature's brutality might be temporary, but it's necessary and admirable, and all the more exquisite because it's ephemeral. The sheer beauty and force of Paglia's prose is mesmerizing, but intellectually, it's all numbingly predictable.

Still, even today, when Paglia talks about art, I pay attention. So few thinkers treat art with such unequivocal reverence—a position I understand and share to a degree, given how much an appreciative posture towards art is inevitably grounded in uncritical acceptance of the normative biases that inform it. But, for better or worse, I've never relinquished the idea of art as holy, as something ensconced in a realm that ultimately transcends society and politics. So Paglia's ritual homages to art are like occasional trips to church or temple: necessary reminders of the cosmos beyond, and of the particular faith tradition—the religion of Art—I have been called to serve.

There are two specific passages from *Sexual Personae* that I credit for converting me, at seventeen, to Pagliaism. The first is the paragraph that concludes the incendiary (for ardent anti-essentialists, at least) first chapter:

> The moment there is imagination, there is myth. We may have to accept an ethical cleavage between imagination and reality, tolerating horrors, rapes and mutilations in art that we would not tolerate in society. For art is our message from the beyond, telling us what nature is up to ... Let us see art for what it is and nature for what it is. From remotest antiquity, western art has seen a parade of sexual personae, emanations of absolutist western mind. Western art is a cinema of sex and dreaming. Art is form struggling to wake from the nightmare of nature.

I read this passage as a blessing—that is, permission—to be, as an artist, fearless, almost to the point of sociopathy. For I saw myself as a card-carrying member of an elite whose task was to deliver ugly truths in the rarefied container of art. Indeed, I strove for an "absolutist western mind," a mind that would know everything there was to know, eternally looking to expand its dominion and power.

Which leads me to the second conversion-causing passage: "Male homosexuality played a ... catalytic role in Renaissance Florence and Elizabethan London. At such moments, male bonding enjoys an amorous intensity of self-assurance, a transient conviction of victory over mothers and nature. For 2,500 years, western culture has fed itself on the enormous achievement of homosexual hybris, small bands of men attaining visionary heights in a few concentrated years of exaltation and defiance." These words provided the ultimate justification I sought for my function in the world as an artist and queer person. I emerged from *Sexual Personae* a bona fide convert, a slave to Western culture, colonized to the marrow.

May 16, 2008

Played a home version of Jeopardy *at [my friend] C's party tonight. I won both games, comfortably. I know it's silly and stupid and shallow and meaningless, but it's good to know that I can at least pull out the brainiac mask when I need it. God knows I'm good for nothing else.*

I was also impressed and inspired by Paglia's professional resilience. After earning her PhD from Yale, she landed a job at Bennington College, where she was the faculty's only open lesbian. Her unfashionable views on gender and sexuality made her numerous enemies within the faculty, leading to her eventual resignation from the college. This was followed by many years during which she struggled to get employment and had to rely, at times, on food stamps to survive. But she soldiered on, finally landing a publisher for *Sexual Personae* after seven failed attempts, in 1990. So the book's breathtaking commercial and critical success was a revenge fantasy come true, a triumph narrative that no aspiring intellectual or wayward outsider could possibly resist.

(Voice Proper is obsessing over the chintzy "philosophizing" of a neoconservative woman while fellow queers are being killed in Jamaica and Yemen. Is it any surprise Paglia's book was a success? Re-inscribing sexual and gender clichés is a surefire way to gain mainstream popularity.)

December 4, 2009

X is in town again. He emailed me yesterday to say he was arriving this morning. Here for a few days for some academic conference. I phone him long distance as soon as I read his email—probably should have feigned nonchalance and not seemed so eager, but I can't lie when it comes to X, coz God help me—I adore him like no other.

We spent most of today together—he fucked me three times. It was as though he never left me or the room in my body he'd opened up, a room I kept untouched 'til the day he returned. Calmly, ruthlessly, he reclaimed what was his.

(Hark, is that Maria Callas singing "Un bel di vedremo" *["One Fine Day"], the famous aria from that most Orientalist of artworks,* Madame Butterfly?*)*

How did X change my life? A sexy intellectual (something that to me only Europeans seemed to know how to pull off), he was handsome but not ostentatious or preening in the stereotypical queer way. He had a decent body but nothing that would get attention in a Davie Street bar. He was completely masculine but not self-consciously or affectedly so. He was well read, a polymath even, but never pedantic or pretentious. While I laboured through the likes of Paglia and, later, Susan Sontag, as part of my perennial effort to self-improve, X changed my life by doing nothing in particular but be himself. He possessed that incandescent trait that people seem to either be born with or acquire only after years of hardship and introspection: insouciance. For the longest time, I, colonized dupe that I was, thought it impossible to find this quality in North America, because our continent is too young; only Europe, with its millennia of history, could spawn the blasé and wise. It was my belief that I, like Paglia and Sontag, *did*, and then some; whereas X, born in the country that birthed Western culture, simply *was*.

(*Although it would be easier to attribute Voice Proper's long disregard for the contributions and achievements—the very experience and existence—of the Indigenous peoples of Turtle Island, and the rest of the globe, to his ignorance and unwillingness to educate himself, we must place the blame where it belongs: to the particular knowledge machine that facilitated this ignorance and unwillingness in the first place, a machine that both explicitly and implicitly supports white supremacy and Western-centricism at every turn. Even his put-down of himself as a "colonized dupe" must be seen in the proper light, as indicative of an individualist approach to what is actually a collective dilemma.*

Also: there's an argument to be made that it was non-white Egypt, not white Greece, that birthed Western culture.)

October 9, 2011

[Notes in preparation for a promotional interview for my play Falling in Time*]*

1. Connect thought process with speech muscles—they are one indivisible whole.

2. Look slightly bored.

3. Look interviewer up and down at various points, like you're analyzing him.

4. Limit your hand movements—remember, you are marmoreal.

5. See if you can find your fedora, and if you do, wear it.

6. Use your chest voice and chew your words like they're precious edible jewels.

7. Find opportunities to use the following words:

- "Poesis"
- "Efficacious"
- "Byzantine"
- "Peripatetic"

8. When in doubt, channel Plato, or Thomas Aquinas, or Erasmus—or at least Sontag.

It was through Paglia that I first heard about Susan Sontag. Paglia made passing (negative) reference to her in an interview on Canadian television, and shortly afterwards, an entire essay on Sontag appeared in Paglia's third book, *Vamps & Tramps*. It was this essay, even more than her too-often obnoxious public persona, that diminished my admiration for Paglia. Childish and self-aggrandizing, the essay's sole purpose seemed to be to trash Sontag and champion its author as the new doyenne of American thought. There was also, partly, the pain of self-reflection: as I recognized these same self-aggrandizing tendencies in myself, witnessing it in others was squirm-inducing.

Still, this piece proved invaluable because it introduced me to Sontag's work. I bought *Against Interpretation* and began a mentorship that ultimately proved more durable than what I had with Paglia. Sontag is the guiding spirit of this book.

Against Interpretation is less than half the length of *Sexual Personae* but contains at least three times the intellectual texture and nuance. The range Sontag displays in this book—her first essay collection and arguably most powerful work—is striking: from Plato to Simone Weil, from Ionesco to sci-fi films, from the French New Wave to interdisciplinary "happenings" (a precursor of sorts to the multimedia collective creations for which Vancouver is renowned), from theoretical essays challenging moralism in art to ones extolling style and celebrating camp. This book is a sleek amalgam of seeming opposites: coldness and pathos, the classical and the modern, low culture and high, the American and the European.

My favourite essay is "Notes on Camp." That it was the first piece of writing to put what is essentially queer taste at the centre of serious discussion has already been much written about; what I will highlight instead is the link Sontag draws between queers and Jews, for it was this passage that, on first reading, most resonated with me: "Not all liberals are Jews, but Jews have shown a particular affinity for liberal and reformist causes. So, not all homosexuals have Camp taste. But homosexuals, by and large, constitute the vanguard—and the most articulate audience—of Camp. (The analogy is not frivolously chosen. Jews and homosexuals are the outstanding creative minorities in contemporary urban culture. Creative, that is, in the truest sense: they are creators of sensibilities. The two pioneering forces of modern sensibility are Jewish moral seriousness and homosexual aestheticism and irony.)" At the time, I adored this passage because the territory it covers in eighty-five words is astonishing: morality and politics, subcultural commentary and aesthetics. And, yes, it happens to legitimize a community to which I belong. I now see these generalizations as extremely problematic, but, just like Paglia's misogynistic statements about queer men, at the time I found them fiercely empowering.

I eagerly sought out her other essay collections. Both *Styles of Radical Will* and *Under the Sign of Saturn* are, in my opinion, superior to *Against Interpretation*—even more probing, closely reasoned, erudite, difficult. Her essay on Ingmar Bergman's *Persona* is a virtual clinic in deep-tissue formalist film analysis. And in these books she introduced me to European thinkers such as Barthes, Canetti, Benjamin, and Cioran; it was in this respect that Sontag was most invaluable to me as a mentor, opening up a world of thoughts and ideas that would have otherwise remained too abstruse for a North American poseur like me to tackle.

As for my stance on the Paglia/Sontag rivalry: although Sontag is not, in my opinion, quite the prose stylist Paglia is, she more than compensates by holding space for complexity and paradox, and by not resorting, for the sake of spice, to inflammatory generalizations and shock value. (Major exception: when she called the white race "the cancer of human history.") Sontag was the logical next step in my intellectual evolution: Paglia embraced simplistic, essentialist, and conservative socio-political and gender theories, and was a passionate defender of Western high art; Sontag was as passionate an apologist for the latter but posited far less colonized and more progressive political views.

However, as you'll see, even Sontag I've had to let go of altogether.

(The cancer metaphor: hyperbolic, but the core message is accurate. Euro-American culture has been the most destructive force on the planet. To claim otherwise is to deny reality, and to argue that other races would have been just as destructive had they possessed the technology and won the wars is conjecture and deflection of the highest order.

Voice Proper's admiration of Sontag's linking queers to Jews: this is as troubling as the seeming innocuousness of his idolizing female thinkers. Is he fully aware of the particular matrices in which women—and Jews, for that matter—develop their intellectual and creative lives? Or the specific barriers both women and Jews must overcome to succeed in an anti-Semitic and patriarchal society? All this is being erased as women and Jews become mere tools for his own personal development.)

My first exposure to Sontag's public persona was in 2010, when I came across a video online of an appearance she made at the San Francisco Public Library just a few years before her death to promote her final novel, *In America*, for which she had just won the National Book Award. After reading from it, she talks reverently and modestly about the writing life—specifically, the purpose of art ("It's impersonal or transpersonal ... something like salvation. I precisely am not confined to being myself through writing—it's a way of being in touch and connected with much larger realities") and what motivates her to write ("It's an act of gratitude as much as an act of emulation. I think a writer is first of all a reader. My deepest motivation for wanting to be a writer and wanting to be a good writer and wanting to be a better writer is the ecstasy I have had as a reader"). Although by this time I had started my

long-overdue embrace of left-wing and identity politics (my early conservatism was, I now realize, completely the result of youthful abstract ideating;
real-life financial, racial, and mental health challenges awakened me, finally,
to the necessity of state-led alleviation of human fragility), Sontag reminded
me that although art exists on a plane that may subsume the problems of self
and world, it ultimately transcends them.

(*Art is dangerous, but not because of the "truths" that Paglia and Sontag speak
of. Art encourages idleness, and human beings are lazy. Idleness over action is
collective death.*)

That Sontag's private personality, by most accounts, often didn't match the
humility and wisdom of her public statements only augmented her aura by
humanizing it. The self-declared "besotted aesthete" came—as I did—from
a completely unintellectual family; apparently, conversations at the dining
table consisted mostly of drivel. Growing up she felt profoundly unlistened
to, and those close to her say that her legendary drive stemmed from a need
for revenge. This is key to understanding her "radical will" (to quote from
the title of one of her best books) to self-transform, to become a great writer,
to be, in her words, "exemplary." She became besotted with great art and
literature, as it offered an escape from her unhappy family life, as did, at age
fifteen, acceptance to the University of Chicago's renowned Hutchins College
for gifted students, which was probably the closest thing America had at the
time to Plato's Academy. Perhaps the most revealing excerpt from her published journals—which are extraordinary in their revelation of the mammoth
insecurities underlying her coolly arrogant persona—is the following short
dialogue she initiates with herself:

> "I want to be good."
> "Why?
> "I want to be what I admire."
> "Why don't you want to be what you are?"

Even after she published *Against Interpretation* and attained world recognition, Sontag felt inadequate and like she never belonged, neither to the

New York literary intelligentsia in which she seemed firmly ensconced nor the larger international sphere of elite writers and thinkers. She harboured a lifelong disdain for anti-intellectual America and, indeed, for being American, claiming in her journals that she wished to "self-Europeanize." The flip side of mammoth insecurity is, of course, megalomania, as evidenced by her frankly stated wish to reach the heights of the Russian masters: "The task is to be as good as D[ostoyevsky]—as serious spiritually, and then go from there."

In her early forties, she was diagnosed with stage-four breast cancer; that she writes so little about it in her journals is further testament to her refusal to cave in to the merely personal. To the astonishment of all—except perhaps herself—she survived that cancer; after surviving a second bout in her late sixties, she died from a third bout at age seventy-one. Still, to survive and thrive for three decades after specialists declared her death imminent was an astonishing manifestation of radical will—a phrase I repeat because it so succinctly sums up what she was all about. That her final cancer was so agonizing mostly because of her flat refusal to accept death—which she equated with obliteration and was therefore out of the question—is chillingly apropos given the overarching aim of her life: to *matter*, in all senses of the word.

Despite my recent discovery of the profound importance of letting go, radical will is still, I think, my single strongest asset: against the odds, it has helped me be *seen*.

April 9, 2011

> [In Manhattan visiting X.]
>
> Arrived in NYC this morning. As Nathan in QAF would say, "I'm doing it. I'm really doing it." Right in the thick of the grandest, most hallowed city on earth—not Brooklyn, not Queens, but Manhattan, pure Manhattan. I'm jetlagged, slept all day, so will likely be up most of the night. Perfect opportunity to start my Emily Dickinson project then: to copy out, with unwavering intention, every line of her every poem, in an effort to absorb at least some of her thought process, and create new neural pathways in the exquisite likeness of hers.

Just got back from a late dinner with X. He's fast asleep now while I write this. Over dinner I found myself studying him—didn't intend to, but it just happened. Everything about him is organic, unadulterated grace. I watched how he picked up his fork, how he turned his wine glass back and forth, how he cut his meat, how he placed food in his mouth. Most of all, what captivated me is how he looked at the menu: with an air of dispassionate passion, of unattached, clinical lust. He had joy for what was offered, but what was offered didn't define him. It remained firmly objects that didn't threaten his subjective integrity. It was the same look he has when he's in bed with me, like he's objectifying and collecting. The exchange is on his terms; I'm willing to be collected.

Whatever he's drinking, I want some. It would make life so much easier.

AIDS and Its Metaphors was one of the last of Sontag's books I got around to reading. It was 2008—I was seeing a therapist for my OCD, and as part of my treatment he mandated me to deliberately expose myself to things I feared. As AIDS remained one of my biggest *bêtes noires*, he advised me to do everything short of having unprotected sex with an HIV-positive person: volunteer for an AIDS organization, go to an AIDS hospice, commemorate World AIDS Day, read a book about AIDS. Unwilling to branch too far out of my comfort zone, I chose option four.

From the book's first words, Sontag's imperious, unwaveringly rational voice assuaged my fears. She leans into the frightening subject matter with unbending intellectual composure, never relenting at any point from what would be justified expressions of grief (Sontag lost a swath of friends and colleagues to the epidemic). The book is a tour de force of rigorous, clear-headed thinking, with Sontag deploying her intellect like a monarch wielding her sceptre. The courage she displays in subjecting to such unsparing analysis what Paglia calls "malevolent nature"—embodied in this case by fatal disease—is intoxicating and, to me when I first read it, empowering. For it was intellect in action as trailblazer to truth, stay against irrational fear, salvation.

Synchronistically, I read the book at around the same time I discovered Buddhism, whose insistence on gently reversing our propensity to impose meaning on what is inherently meaningless—that is, everything—dovetailed well with the book's modus operandi: to alleviate the public's AIDS phobia, caused, Sontag argues, by clumsy but widespread thinking that linked the disease—and disease in general—to immorality and sexual depravity, courtesy of centuries-old metaphors generated by religion and medicine. She acknowledges that, "of course, one cannot think without metaphors. But that does not mean there aren't some metaphors that we might as well abstain from or try to retire."

Here was an intellectual giant—a model of the queer serious—who was cautioning against blanket, all-or-nothing thinking. As a chronic catastrophizer, I found this simple admonition liberating. It was also a direct challenge to her (and my) old hero Thomas Mann, who in *Death in Venice* made disease replete with metaphor.

Also liberating was the following link she draws between AIDS phobia and cultural conservatism: "The behaviour AIDS is stimulating is part of a larger, grateful return to what is perceived as 'conventions,' like the return to figure and landscape, tonality and melody, plot and character, and other much vaunted repudiations of difficult modernism in the arts ... The response to AIDS, while in part perfectly rational, amplifies a widespread questioning that had been rising in intensity throughout the 1970s of many of the ideals (and risks) of enlightened modernity; and the new sexual realism goes with the rediscovery of the joys of tonal music, Bouguereau, a career in investment banking, and church weddings."

To be AIDS phobic, then, was to be a philistine, a reactionary. I had no interest in being either. It was Susan Sontag, not an AIDS hotline, that helped me finally overcome my AIDS phobia.

(Queer activists were hostile to AIDS and Its Metaphors *upon its release, and it's easy to see why. Sontag's approach is so anemic it's dead; her exquisite intellectualizing is the stuff of Nero—what was most needed in 1989 was a call to action. But what can we expect from a woman who was never publicly queer in her lifetime, afraid that coming out would affect not only her credibility but*

her attractiveness to the heteronormative men who comprised a large part of her readership? An overly impassioned and polemical AIDS book would have, she probably feared, blown her cover.

That Voice Proper admires her so is not surprising, given her European pretensions to being a "universalist"—beyond gender, race, and sexuality. Paglia, in a rare moment of sanity, was correct in describing her as "Miss Mandarin in her New York apartment"—a haughty, effete brainiac out of touch with the real world.)

I found solace and inspiration in both Sontag's and Paglia's personal trajectories—their unabashed stridency, their single-minded belief in their vocation. Ostracization, poverty, illness—none of these hurdles could derail them from leading an intellectual and creative life. I share their pig-headedness: neither lack of family wealth (which a number of my friends and colleagues have, making it easier for them to pursue typically low-earning artistic careers), nor a couple of mental breakdowns (precipitated at least in part by the financial and emotional insecurity caused by working in undernourished ecologies such as writing and theatre), nor a few stints on welfare have convinced me to follow any other possible career path. Just as I am brown and queer, I am an artist, period. No counter-argument from the hegemony can alter what is a hard fact: that, like Paglia and Sontag, I am besotted by art, and good for little else.

(Too much liberal-individualist whining here in lieu of a critique of systemic undervaluation of art and artists.)

April 15, 2011

[In Manhattan visiting X.]

Having coffee in X's kitchen this morning, I'm suddenly seized by self-contempt.

I don't like myself. I never have.

X loving me all week, when I haven't lifted a finger, haven't rehearsed the parts I'm playing, haven't pre-thought all the astute things I'm going to say. Loving me for me, he's yanked the ground from under me.

I hate him as much as I love him. Doesn't he ever need anything more than his own skin?

(It requires some privilege to just "be oneself." It's easier for some than others to "just be themselves." X is white, cis, straight-passing (bi-identified to boot) and upper middle class—of course it's less arduous for him to "be himself" than for folks like Paglia, Sontag, Voice Proper, all of whom started with far fewer advantages, which probably goes a long way to explaining why all three of them were, or are, so uncomfortable with themselves and therefore so strident.)

Sontag suggests in *Against Interpretation* that the realm of intellectual perfection is, finally, not something we can fully access. But perhaps the ideal of it, for both personal and social purposes, is worth preserving.

Or is it? Not too long ago I'd arrived at the conclusion that it wasn't, that it was little more than a tool of the white male hegemony to retain at least even a symbolic hold on a fast-diversifying society. But the wholesale rejection and disdain I saw displayed by some of my New Left colleagues for *anything* generated by a white male, living or dead—often without having read, seen, or listened to the work—struck me as being in line with the vulgar, predictable "intellectualism" I'd come to tire of in Paglia.

Again, it was Sontag who helped me through this conundrum—she reminded me of the importance of nuance and texture, thereby allowing me to take the best parts of the New Left while discarding its more unfortunate aspects. I now happily embrace a much more diverse brew of artworks than I used to: works by people of colour, Indigenous people, women and gender non-binary people, as well as works from pop culture (a quarter-century after their flourishing, I have become a devoted fan of grunge rock, namely Nirvana and Hole).

But the standards I use to evaluate *any* work are, for lack of a better word, classical—and by that term I certainly don't mean a "repudiation of difficult modernism." Indeed, what I mean by "classical" is the upholding of any standards at all—specifically, the refusal to accept any artifact as qualitatively indistinguishable from another (i.e., the notion that an episode of *Full House* is as artistically valuable as *Hamlet*). Doubtless, this will displease some of my fellow progressives, but I was reared on the idea of art as something set apart, transcendent, magical; for me to go deep into an artwork, it must work magic on me. Certainly, one of the benefits of self-decolonizing is that I now find magic in far more artworks than I used to, which has added more texture, subtlety, and, yes, joy to my daily life.

So I'm as besotted (perhaps more so) an aesthete as ever, and I credit Sontag for showing me the benefits of an aesthetic life. But although I remain an admirer, I've had to officially let go of her as a role model. I'm glad I imbibed her teachings on art's transpersonality, but it's time for me to ground precisely in what was bypassed on that transpersonal path—crucial questions of race, class, and sexual identity, questions Sontag rarely dealt with in her own work and certainly never in the context of her own positionality, preferring to see herself as pure consciousness and, therefore, beyond identity. To exist and function, simultaneously, in both the worldly realm and the transcendent one, to honour the struggle while charting a path beyond it: this is the task of the doubly melancholic artist.

(Speaking of letting go, can we let go, once and for all, of the word "diverse"? It has colonized that which we must identify with much greater specificity. So, for example, the new order towards which we should all be working is not one with more "diversity"—which could very possibly keep the old system going, with simply more "diverse" people running it—but rather one in which the imperialist white supremacist capitalist patriarchy [bell hooks's term] ceases to be.

As for artistic "standards"—let's remember that racism and misogyny are also informed by "standards." Why give art a free pass? Is it always inherently more benign? So instead of "standards," why can't Voice Proper just speak of "taste," or of some works "resonating" with him more than others?)

Paglia and Sontag were stepping stones to more rarefied intellectual role models. Sontag led me to Theodor Adorno, who argued in opaquely biting aphorisms that avant-garde art and Marxist economics go hand in hand. And then came three sexually nonconforming thinkers who spoke to my positionalities as writer, mental health patient, and queer person.

Ludwig Wittgenstein delves into the nature of language, first conceiving it—in *Tractatus Logico-Philosophicus*—as something that could accurately and faithfully capture the objective world, then doing an about-face at the end of his career by arguing—in the posthumous *Philosophical Investigations*—that language has multiple uses, all socially inflected, and is by no means a container of pictures of external reality. The courage to self-critique and change his mind I found empowering, and his final position I deemed in concord with the Buddhist and Sontagian ideas with which I was enamoured. In addition, this position is a direct continuation of that predominantly queer line of thinking that originated in ancient Greece and continued through Pater, Symonds, and Wilde, positing art (in the most general sense) as detached from external reality, representing only itself.

Then came Michel Foucault. I had avoided Foucault for far too long, largely because Paglia wrote so disparagingly of him, so when I read *Madness and Civilization* and loved it, my days as even a wavering Paglia acolyte were over. Whatever historical inaccuracies the book is guilty of—and it has been accused of many—are, to me, moot; it's an epically eviscerating tract against the brutal oppressiveness of social structures, and a liberatory plea for tolerance of the weird, the eccentric, the different. Reading it made me recall why I'd never forgiven Mr Z for calling the authorities on me.

Finally, Judith Butler. Next to Heidegger, Butler is the most difficult thinker I have ever read, so when I reached the last paragraph of *Gender Trouble*, I treated myself to champagne. Part of the thrill, I concede, had to do with lingering egomania—I was proud that her obscurantist prose did not completely befuddle me. But the larger part of the thrill was her theory of performativity: specifically, how each repeated performance of an identity is, partly, an attempt to ward off anxiety—an idea that resonated with me because of my lifelong personal insecurities and recent introduction to identity politics. Indeed, it is in this Butlerian context that I call this book "a performance."

Wittgenstein, Foucault, and Butler provide disruptions to conventional thought, and are examples of a long line of oppositional ideating that the queer community has been instrumental in shaping. These three writers helped make me a critical thinker: they gave me permission to question even the most ostensibly self-evident truths.

I'm aware they're all white. I'm also aware that becoming theoretically savvy is an entry to yet another (white, middle-class) elite. And I wonder about the myriad ways I perpetuate elitism, so ingrained is it in the way I stave off anxiety.

(Why exactly does he need "permission" to undertake the questioning of which he speaks?)

April 17, 2011

Just left NYC. On the plane back home.

We fucked before I left. Rough and fast and dirty.

Afterwards we talked. He called our connection intense, that it was intense from the moment we met.

I tensed up, felt really uncomfortable. So I started nerding out about Shostakovich.

He said I don't need to impress him. He told me to be still and breathe.

In a roundabout way, I told him I loved him. Why am I always the first to break?

To this day, he has yet to break. And I'm still learning how to be still.

7 | DIVINE: MARIA CALLAS

It was Paglia that nudged this Filipinx queer boy towards self-acceptance in his late teens. The ego-consolidation and self-affirmation of a newly out university sophomore.

April 5, 1994

Homosexuality = shamanism = the chosen = antennae of the world.

Art points skyward, defies nature, transcends the muck. It is, without question, the highest human faculty.

But despite discovering Buddhism not long after, with its emphasis on ego-devaluation and selflessness, the ideas in the journal entry from that time—about striving, achieving, perpetually self-improving—are still with me. They still, to a large extent, motor my existence.

———————

There is no greater model for perpetual self-improvement than Maria Callas, the most celebrated operatic soprano of the twentieth century. She was called La Divina—the Divine One. Most modern classical music stars dwell in rarefied peaks, free from the glare of the masses, subjects of esoteric study. Maria Callas was an exception. She was a pre-Stonewall icon, the queer cultural intelligentsia's Judy Garland. To adore Callas in the twenty-first century is, in a way, to regress to that pre-Stonewall age, when queer men, in retreat from a world that hated them, found solace in the perfection of art. Which is half the reason for this essay: to reconnect with the divine, where, as Callas explained in an interview, "everything is harmony."

But this essay is also about grounding in the worldly realm, where the norm is *dis*harmony, inequality, injustice, where the only way through is struggle. True social justice is not—should not—be easy, for it requires the wholesale questioning of old assumptions and modes of thinking. My guides on this journey have been bell hooks, Cornel West, and angel Kyodo williams.

They have more in common with Callas than one might think.

August 28, 2014

D and I finally slept together last night. He's a beautiful man, physically, mentally, emotionally—he fucks like someone who's come through the fire on the other side; in other words, with gratitude, gentleness, soul. Whatever nerves I had vanished coz I don't have to pretend with him. Now, it's the morning after and none of my fears have surfaced.

My first openly poz lover. No fanfare, just fun. No trumpets, just tenderness.

An older, well-off white guy—don't know what my QTBIPOC friends will say about this, some of whom, on principle, have gone off white guys altogether. All I know is that he's a change of pace—and his ex is white, so he's not a fetishizer.

After we fucked we talked about opera; like me, he's a Callas shipper. I tell him that the next time we hook up I'll bring my box set of Callas's complete studio recordings and either analyze them or screw to them, all night long.

La bohème was my favourite opera once upon a time, but I eventually tired of it, coming to see it as "opera lite." But surfing YouTube many years ago, I happened across an audio recording of Mimi's act 1 aria rendered by Callas, a singer I'd never particularly cared for. From my laptop, her voice emerged—that bottled, naked sound that has always divided opinion. Two and a half minutes in, the aria swelled towards its high point: "*Ma quando vien lo sgelo, il primo sole é mio.*" The simple, virginal Mimi singing of how spring's first kiss is hers. Callas and orchestra in perfect synchronicity as the great Greek American diva, for a moment, lifts the veils from sensuality, and a stodgy, effete art form becomes a container for living truth. I've listened to other Mimis—Tebaldi,

Scotto, Stratas—but none achieve the miracle that Callas pulls off. I'm not hyperbolizing when I call my Callas moment one of existential clarity, when my East met my West, when finally there was equilibrium.

So began my personal study—one undertaken, so it seems, by many other queer men—of the life and art of Maria Callas: ugly duckling, musical genius. Although she wasn't queer (at least as far as anyone knows), the narrative of her life—informed by egomania, willpower, metamorphosis, sexual frustration and fulfillment, and, finally, tragedy—certainly was: the lonely outsider who pays the price for professional and personal acceptance. But the most efficient manifestation of her queerness is her art, a masterpiece drawn from imperfection, insecurity, and a bit of hate.

(Again, the narrator should deploy the term "gay" rather than "queer." Callas is an icon to a particular faction of the queer community: mostly white, middle-class, university-educated gay males.)

Callas's voice takes me inside myself and out again—the exact opposite of what happens when I listen to a more conventionally beautiful voice. The latter is escapism—a fireworks display from which I return unchanged. The Callas voice is too flawed, too human for escape: the dark, eerie timbre; the deep, ferocious chest tones; the bottled middle register; and the forced and wobbly high notes (especially later in her career) were the musical equivalents of her personal flaws and, in turn, mine. Her mentor, the conductor Tullio Serafin, christened her *La grande vociaccia*—the Great Ugly Voice—but it was ugliness that accessed and embodied the divine. The impeccable diction, the flawless weighing of every note, the silken ornamentations, the perfectly placed slides from one note to another—her great ugly voice both subsumed the world and transcended it.

It was, in short, a voice from the closet.

You know the story—it's *my* story. Bullied and ostracized, the young queer boy strives to be the best at whatever he's good at. Not the best he can be but "the best," period. Just as society invokes "objective standards" in condemning his burgeoning sexuality, so the young queer boy invokes them in his quest for perfection. Callas attracts a lot of queer men because she's the best, period.

And she became the very best despite a bevy of disadvantages: a broken home, a difficult mother, a figure deemed ungainly, a seemingly untamable voice. In *The Queen's Throat*, his brilliant and now-legendary paean to opera, Wayne Koestenbaum writes, "The listener's body is illuminated, opened up: a singer doesn't expose her own throat, she exposes the listener's interior." When I listen to Callas, every trill, every flourish becomes a journey out of the dregs, a manifestation of her personal triumphs and, by extension, mine. In her unflinching artistry, I see my own obsessive-compulsive perfectionism; in her mid-career weight loss, my metamorphosis to muscle-bound quasi Adonis.

Scholastic excellence was my weapon growing up, as was success as a classical pianist and, later, acclaim as a writer. Egos that are mutilated eventually balloon, and for most of my life it's been egomania that's gotten me up in the morning, a narcissistic search for vengeance against a world that I was convinced was against me.

I adore Callas because she avenges on my behalf. She is me when she transforms herself to meet society's beauty standards and conquer, wholesale, both opera fans and the general public. Each diamond-pointed gruppetto, every sweeping arpeggio, is an act of revenge against queer bashers, against all who ever crossed me. Indeed, Callas's own words in interviews, "We [artists] must whip ourselves into shape like a soldier," and "I would not kill my enemies, but I will make them get down on their knees," suggest a militaristic, score-settling approach to her craft.

Her 1949 career breakthrough was one of the queerest events in twentieth-century opera. While performing Brünnhilde in Wagner's *Die Walküre*, she was asked, on a few days' notice, to fill in for a sick colleague who was to sing Elvira in Bellini's *I puritani*, a part Callas had never before performed. To perform, back to back, a Wagner opera—which features heavy orchestration and demands power and stamina from the singer—and a bel canto one—with its minimal orchestration and demands for nimbleness and floridity—was an unheard of feat, akin to a skater speed skating one week and figure skating the next. She opened as Elvira to an incredulous audience. This was Callas at her queerest: doing the unthinkable, defying categories.

Breaking the seemingly impenetrable wall between the Wagnerian repertoire and the Italian bel canto one, Callas—despite her self-declared aesthetic conservatism—was a bona fide postmodern opera star: convention-busting, boundary-blurring, *sui generis*.

There is also the curious quality of Callas's sexual persona. There was an affected, contrived quality to her famously genteel way of moving and speaking, a quality undercut by the unaffectedly fierce, "masculine" manner in which she approached her work. Unlike her alleged archrival, the musically demure and unthreatening Renata Tebaldi, Callas attacked the music with a decisiveness normally associated with male singers. The result was the kind of persona that would make Paglia's heart flutter: solipsistic, hermaphroditic, narcissistic, self-completing.

And there is the story of how Maria's nunlike devotion to her calling ended when she met shady Greek shipping magnate Aristotle Onassis. The virginal high priestess of opera had lived most of her life in her throat; the extraordinarily sexual Onassis opened her up to the rest of her body, a body she'd hated, a body that, for most of her life, nobody had ever wanted.

———————————

Opera is pre-modern, steeped in the past, home to myth, old-style melodrama, and stereotypical notions of sex and gender. If opera remains popular, even outside queerdom, it has little to do with the inner (i.e., plot lines) and almost everything to do with the outer (i.e., the music, the staging).

When queers love Callas, as I do, they are embracing pre-modernism while queering it up royally. For she dragged hidden human truths out of sexist, archaic stories—out of the effete, rococo, centuries-old closet that is opera. Absolute honesty is queer; notions of normalcy are always relative. Callas simultaneously embraced the norms of bel canto singing and broke through them to illuminate the complexities of human emotion. She was the most profoundly gifted vocal artist of her century, one whose polychromatic voice could encapsulate every nuance and sub-nuance of feeling. There is no irony in worshipping Callas, as there is with Garland or Monroe—when queers align themselves with Callas, they align themselves with greatness. But it is greatness haunted by the omnipresence of the abyss, by intimations of what can and, in Callas's case, did go wrong. The great Callas scholar—and avowed opera queen—John Ardoin likens the experience of listening to Callas to watching a trapeze act. Usually there is a net below, but in those rare instances when there is not, a completely different atmosphere is created. "The very being of each spectator seems to be bound up in each step taken on high," says Ardoin in *The Callas Legacy*, "for there is no longer any semblance of pretense."

Callas's vocal fall was legendary, ugly. Her hard-won artistic victories were Pyrrhic—unequalled greatness for a too-brief time. Pushing her voice beyond its natural range, tackling the most technically intimidating repertoire, giving every ounce of herself to each and every performance, she seemed constitutionally incapable of performing with a net. And although this cost Callas her voice (her singing career was over by age forty-two), it is what gave her singing its abyss-defying, life-and-death intensity.

But she could never escape the abyss—indeed, she seemed always to be staring it down. Her singing, even at its most technically brilliant, never sounded easy, the way the vocalizing of her great bel canto rivals Joan Sutherland and Montserrat Caballé did. It always carried with it a knowledge of the fragility of greatness—and of the unspeakable horrors that lurk beneath it. That Callas had to work to access the divine is what gave her art its stirringly human dimension.

It comforts me that even one of the most celebrated thinkers on race and gender can hold space for the divine. In a lecture she gave at St. Norbert's College in 2017 as part of the Agape Latte Speaker Series, bell hooks said, "I consider that I practice a visionary feminism that is, in fact, completely informed by my faith. It keeps me from having some notion than men are bad and women are good. It keeps me on the transcendent path, knowing that we are always more than our race, our gender, our sexual practice, that we are, in fact, transcendent spirit."

Around the time I got deep into Callas—which was while I was recovering from my breakdown—I also discovered African American thinkers—to wit, hooks, Cornel West, and angel Kyodo williams. Models of intellectual, visionary activism, they marry theoretical sophistication with the sky-piercing soulfulness of the gospel music in the churches in which they were reared. I concede that my initial impetus towards them was born largely of guilt: as a racialized person approaching mid-life, I realized that virtually all my intellectual role models were white. So I studied these authors with the same ferocity as I had E.M. Forster, Tennessee Williams, Thomas Mann, Susan Sontag. They provided the final ingredient in my philosophical maturation: a profound awareness of social injustice, and a fiery passion to correct it. This epoch in my life—which I affectionately call my Shirley Verrett phase (Verrett was the renowned African American soprano critics dubbed "the Black Callas")—set the stage for some of the most active years of my professional career. While I was artistic director of Vancouver's professional queer-mandated theatre company, I branched out of my personal comfort zone and became an outspoken and well-known local and national advocate for greater cultural inclusiveness in theatre. Inevitably, running a theatre company moved my focus outwards; to my own astonishment, I was able to transcend (at least to a degree) the monster that was my ego.

This was also the period when I started identifying—in both speech and writing, and proudly, without even the thought of a sigh or eye-roll—as a "queer, Filipinx writer based in the unceded ancestral territories of the Musqueam, Squamish, and Tsleil-Waututh nations," instead of a "Vancouver-based writer who happens to be gay and Filipino." I completely dropped "gay" as an identifier in favour of the more inclusive and overtly political "queer," as "gay" denotes the white middle-class male milieu in which, I realized, I had been so co-opted. I was neither white nor middle class, and it was time I owned it. To fail to would be to continue both my own and others' erasure—the erasure I should have been fighting all along.

One might say that hooks, West, and williams grounded me in the realities of the worldly realm, whereas Callas transported me to the spiritual one. But this dichotomy is not only simplistic but inaccurate: for hooks, West, and williams, just like Callas, embody, for me, the task of living in both realms at once. Unlike most white leftist intellectuals, hooks, West, and williams are unabashedly spiritual beings (hooks and West are Christians; williams is an ordained Buddhist priest) whose religious faiths motivate their plangent calls for social change. Just as Callas grounded her divine art in earthly imperfection, hooks, West, and williams point their radical politics towards the divine.

(We must take umbrage with "my Shirley Verrett phase," because its origin is in Verrett being dubbed by primarily white critics as "the Black Callas"—which re-inscribes whiteness as the norm and non-whiteness as the exception.

We must also wonder how much this enthusiasm for Black thinkers is informed by a "woke white" take on Blackness—i.e., a romantic view of Black thought as being particularly profound and "savvy" because it ostensibly and invariably stems from suffering and oppression.

Finally, although we can admire this newfound appreciation of Filipinxness, is it right for someone so whitewashed and co-opted to loudly and publicly, in mid-life, reclaim their ethnic heritage? Beware the born-again person of colour; making up for lost time, he's often completely obnoxious.)

The divine. For me—and, I would guess, for lots of other queer men—the divine has primarily taken two forms. The first is art. The second is sex.

"Death ... the opposite ... is desire," says Blanche DuBois—a startlingly prophetic précis of the late-twentieth-century queer male experience, defined as it was by the polarities of erotic fulfillment and deadly disease. Physical love, in the face of sordid, mythopoetical fatality, became even more intense, more transcendent—an act of ecstatic defiance against the ever-present threat of death.

Indeed, early death is the final italicization of queer-icon status. Callas died at fifty-three in her Paris apartment, *sola, perduta, abbandonata*. Onassis, the love of her life, had left her for Jackie Kennedy, and Callas's final world tour betrayed a voice in irrevocable ruins. From *la dolce vita* and unprecedented heights of operatic artistry she had come to this: a recluse wasting away on Quaaludes and memories of a once-glorious voice. Apparently, on her deathbed she had never looked lovelier or more immaculate: undimmed beauty even in her darkest moment. As it was radical will that allowed her to achieve artistic greatness and physical beauty, it was radical will that propelled her to her early, quiet death—if not technically a suicide, then a perfectly paced winding down.

To die beautiful and young is in concord with queerdom's cult of youth, with that familiar refrain of the vain club bunny: "Who wants to die an old queen?"

As for art: Cornel West, in conversation with Steve McQueen at the Whitney Museum in 2016, beautifully encapsulates the challenge for the artist to stay strong in the face of the world's injustice: "I do think that anybody who has the audacity to be an artist has to be on intimate terms with despair ... Anybody who looks candidly, honestly, unflinchingly at the world in which we live has good grounds for suicidal proclivities, if you have a sensitivity to suffering. The question is, can you fortify yourself in such a way that you can transform your sensitivity into a truth-telling, in which the despair is an integral element, but it doesn't have the last word?" The answer, I think, is implicit in his question: by keeping one's eye on "truth-telling"—in other words, art, which can change hearts and minds and outlive us all.

La grande vociaccia. The ugly voice became the instrument of the century's sublimest operatic expression. To mould beauty out of ugliness is the queerest of acts. From channelling deviancy into the creation of polychrome frescoes to transmuting HIV-positive statuses into marks of desirability, queers are often expert alchemists, reliant on magic to survive. In the magic of Callas's music we see the sanctioned version of our own all-too-private narratives, our rowing and striving, our ferociously willed ascents to greatness. Whether these ascents are actualized or merely fantasized is moot; Callas reminds us that, no matter how brilliant we make ourselves, or how accessible become the corridors of power, disaster is always just a stone's throw away.

January 7, 2015

> So D and I listened to the entire Lisbon Traviata *last night [Callas's legendary 1958 Lisbon performance of the Verdi opera, recordings of which for decades were notoriously difficult to find. It subsequently became the overarching and titular symbol of a queer- and AIDS-themed play by Terrence McNally]. Later, he recounted to me how he was introduced to opera.*

"This older guy I had a thing with in Halifax," he said. "I was 18, he was 30, I think. A schoolteacher. Taught me a lot. Extremely cultured, educated, well read. Spoke five languages fluently. Knew a lot about everything. Completely closeted his entire life—just wasn't safe to come out then. And he came from a die-hard Christian family who would have completely disowned him. But Monteverdi, Purcell, bel canto, Verdi, Wagner—opera was his religion. He was completely, utterly devoted to it. He knew every aria, every duet, every overture, everything."

"So Terrence McNally," I quipped. "So white gay male."

"He wasn't white. He was a descendant of runaway slaves. He was black."

(Hyper-culturedness, like hyper-musculature, is usually overcompensation for something. In this case, plainly, it's for shame of being Black, a shame brought upon by our white supremacist society, which is also behind the author's assumption that the man was white.)

I'm quick to anger these days with white people. As aware as I am that it's not individuals but the system that deserves my ire, the system inevitably expresses itself through individuals, and I find myself increasingly impatient with both white fragility and white people's inability to comprehend how they directly benefit from the majority's inherited, ingrained, subconscious white supremacist thinking. Which is why I have such gratitude for people such as angel Kyodo williams, whose thoughts I remind myself of when I begin to feel rage in my body. "With a little awareness of who we are and our shared humanity with others, we can begin to relax a little," she writes in *Being Black: Zen and the Art of Living with Fearlessness and Grace.* Instead of an "Us vs. Them" mentality, which she calls "dangerous and, in all honesty, unrealistic," she asks us to remember that "wherever we are is Our House, and we must all live in this house together."

And, yes, there's art—the other way I overcome anger. The pacifying effect of shifting one's focus to something transcendent and beautiful. But to over-indulge in this is to regress completely to an age of masks, when passion was sublimated, when brilliance was born of suffering. When we revered the likes of Callas because there was no out-and-proud icon to revere.

To align with Callas is to align with pre-Stonewall queers, the closet-dwelling, aesthetic types that queers my age were supposed to have left behind. They brought beauty to the world but did little for social transformation and justice.

I am a proud brown queer man. I do not wish to regress.

But I am attracted to the closet; I cannot and will not deny it completely. This narrow space allotted us we populated with jewels—diamond-pointed representations of our loves, fears, neuroses. I am a citizen but also an aesthete: I hunger for the divine. The Age of the Closet—the Age of Callas—honoured both earth and sky. Queers today, it seems to me, either deny the sky outright, or anemically invoke the sky to avoid necessary earthly struggle.

(The narrator's glorification of the closet verges on the masochistic.

And once again, by appropriating a gifted woman to further a phallocentric narrative, he's caving into a pernicious misogyny masquerading as adoration.

His love affair with the closet is a fetishization of oppression and an affront to progress and social justice.

His claim to being "a proud brown queer man" must be interrogated.)

I want complexity. I want texture. I want beauty.

These love notes to Callas, then, are love notes to the closet, a place that inhibited action but ignited imagination. Where unassuaged pain and suffering were catalysts for great art. Where a voice as queer as Maria Callas's could be called beautiful.

8 | FLIP-FLOP: BEING BROWN

I've never been proud to be Filipinx.

But I've never felt anything about being Filipinx—or, more accurately, have *aimed* to feel nothing. Like right-handedness, flat-footedness, or genetic predisposition to one condition or another, I thought it neither here nor there, an accident of birth. Being queer was different—that, I contended, was a spiritual condition involving one's innermost passions. But Filipinxness was a surface trait, destined, in a utopian future, to be, like whiteness, invisible. And what better way to ensure this future than to never talk about it?

(A surface trait, like a wart, a sleepy eye, or a harelip. Because inside he was as white—if not whiter—than his white friends and lovers.)

April 3, 1988

Last night, Mom forced me to go with her and a claque of other Filipinos to some godforsaken hole-in-the-ground karaoke dump in Surrey or Langley or whatever trash-box suburb that was. I had to endure three-plus hours of Filipinos singing schmaltzy pop dirges, with quality ranging from pretty-decent-for-an-amateur to kill-me-now embarrassingly horrible.

Just as horrible, if not more so, was the utter drivel that passed for conversation the entire night. I don't give a shit if so-and-so are closet lesbians and who the "man" is in the relationship, I don't give a shit how proud C is that [her husband] E was finally able to buy her the diamond ring she always wanted, I don't give a shit that P's white husband left her for the nanny they brought over from the Phils. I want real conversations about real things, about the mind and the spirit, about society and art.

If there's a God, I'll be delivered immediately from this inanity to a sphere where I'll be surrounded by people I can look up to, who inspire me to be who and what I can admire.

The Laguna Copperplate was discovered by a labourer in 1989, near the mouth of the Lumbang River, east of Manila. The labourer sold it to an antique dealer who, in June 1990, sold it to the National Museum of the Philippines. Measuring only twenty centimetres by twenty centimetres (eight inches by eight inches), and covered on one side with a ten-line inscription written in Kawi script (a combination of Old Malay, Old Tagalog, and Sanskrit), it dates, based on the text, to the year 900 BCE. The inscribed text provides conclusive evidence that a sophisticated society with rulers and international trading existed in the Philippines at least six centuries prior to contact with European colonizers.

Before the discovery of the Laguna Copperplate, Filipinx were taught their history began in 1521, the year of Magellan's arrival. Most pre-colonial writing had been done on perishable bamboo, and Spanish missionaries burnt entire collections of documents they deemed pagan.

Spain ruled the Philippines from 1565 to 1898. From 1646 to 1648, this rule was repeatedly and unsuccessfully challenged by the Dutch. In 1762 came the British, who occupied Manila for two years. The Spanish-American War of 1898 ceded control of the country to the Americans, who ruled the Philippines until 1941, when the Japanese seized control of forty percent of the country. The Americans reclaimed complete control in 1944, before Philippine independence was granted in 1946.

Filipinx genocide—1899 to 1913. Three million Filipinx were killed by the Americans after they defeated Spain in the Spanish-American War. US troops were instructed to kill everyone, regardless of gender, over the age of ten, conducting a scorched-earth campaign whereby villages were destroyed and transformed into concentration camps. Anyone caught trying to escape was, without exception, shot.

Filipinx were regarded as little better than dogs. In a letter recounting how he was ordered to kill "every native in sight," an American soldier wrote, "I am probably growing hard-hearted, for I am in my glory when I can sight my gun on some dark skin and pull the trigger."

After praying to God one night, President William McKinley, orchestrator of the genocide, decided it would make good business sense for America to finish what the Spaniards had started but, astonishingly, couldn't complete in their 333 years of rule over the islands: Christianize and civilize the natives, who obviously could not govern themselves.

I had no knowledge of my people's genocide until a few years ago, when I heard Cornel West mention it in a discussion online. My mother said she was taught that Americans were the country's saviours. She was never taught about the genocide in school.

For those much more versed in Filipinx history and culture than I am, this list of invasions and account of genocide is rudimentary, even mundane. But for me it's had the effect of a long-awaited cloud-clearing—an answer to a question that was always there but I could never articulate.

At a Filipinx cultural event I attended recently, in the middle of a demonstration of *arnis*, the national sport and martial art of the Philippines, a practitioner made reference to how Filipinx people are always "running. Running from and running *to*. Just running."

When I was around ten or so, I overheard a conversation Lola was having with a friend in the other room. Someone they knew had just died. From what I could gather, at the precise moment they started talking about him, a fly appeared in the room. Lola observed that the fly was likely the *kaluluwa*—incarnation—of the dead friend. Lola's friend piped up about how Lola's animism was a relic of how stupid we used to be before the Spaniards shook sense into us. The woman was exceedingly eloquent and argued her point with great passion.

I taught piano to an older Filipinx man for a few years. His live-in partner was a wealthy white businessman, so he lived quite well. He met my mother a few times: although she always spoke to him in Tagalog, he would only ever respond in English. (Whenever my mother encountered him he was always alone, never with his partner; furthermore, he was born in Manila and came to Canada when he was forty, so I know he spoke the language.) Once, we were talking about clothes and I mentioned a sale at Sears downtown. Making a face of disgust (genuine, not feigned), he snapped, "I'm a Holt Renfrew boy."

My maternal uncle was a gregarious, generous, kind-hearted veteran of the US Navy. Relatives and friends nicknamed him "White" because of his fair skin. He married and had two children with a Spanish woman, and they divided their time between Virginia and Spain. On one of his visits to Vancouver, he asked for a knife and fork at a Chinese restaurant. "You don't know how to use chopsticks?" I asked. "I do," he answered. "I just choose not to. Knife and fork for me. I'm Spanish American now."

Although my parents separated when I was three, I maintained a relationship (though not a close one) with my father. Once, in my mid-twenties, during one of my father's relatively infrequent visits to Vancouver—he'd moved to Mississauga when I was ten—I spent time with him and his side of the family at one of those suburban all-you-can-eat Chinese buffets that my mother and I—urban snobs with easy access to *real* Chinese food—loved to poke fun at. As it had been awhile since I'd seen my father and his family, they were all stunned by my new buffed, acne-free appearance. My Dad, never one to issue compliments and always somewhat competitive with me, conceded that, yes, I was indeed good-looking, especially compared to most other Filipinos, but added that my brother, Edgar, would have definitely been better looking, because of his fair skin. (Edgar, born two years before me, died when he was a month old.)

My friend, a nurse, told me about a conversation she overheard recently between a white woman's family and hospital staff. The woman had suffered a stroke, and staff asked the family if she needed any home care. "No, we're fine," said one of her children. "We have a Filipino at home."

One of my best friends is a European Canadian who, though politically progressive, gets into many verbal sallies with me about identity politics, which he deems divisive and a distraction from what he feels is the real issue: money. Once, over drinks, he told me that, my brown skin aside, and for all my railings against colonialism and white supremacy, I'm as white as he is. I shrugged and rolled my eyes; secretly, I was flattered.

When one hears "Filipinx" (more likely "Filipino," in general parlance), what does one think of?

- Nannies
- Housekeepers
- Nurses
- Singers (both professional and amateur/karaoke)
- Cast members of various professional and amateur productions of *Miss Saigon*
- Boxers

There is much to admire in being skilled in the caring professions. It's lovely to be able to carry a tune. And as for boxers—well, Pacquiao does look pretty hot without a shirt on.

In my experience, Filipinx tend to be more popular with white people than many other minorities. Popular adjectives used to describe us include "friendly," "warm," "loving," and "nurturing." White people, of course, love that we speak English more or less fluently (English is, for all intents and purposes, the country's primary official language). They praise newly arrived Filipinx on their work ethic—that they typically send most of their earnings back to their families in the Phils never fails to inspire genuine admiration and awe. We're "family-oriented," "dutiful," "self-effacing," "self-sacrificing." We are thought to be loyal. We are not seen as a threat.

Even in the pan-Asian world, Filipinx occupy an odd place. I'm aware that in some surveys in the States, Filipinx are classified not as "Asian" but as "Pacific Islander"; or the term "Asian" is expressly qualified as "including Filipino." In Asia, the racism exercised against Filipinx by the more privileged Asians—to wit, the Japanese, the Chinese, and the Koreans—is well documented; our darker skin, lower economic status, and perceived historical weakness in the face of white imperialists have, it seems, irreparably damaged our brand. Speaking of whiteness, there have been opinions circulating that Asians are "the new white," with the possible exception of the relatively small percentage of us who are ethnically purely Chinese or mestizx/half-white. Filipinx, I suspect, are not included in this formulation.

Notably, there are more than enough examples from history to counter the unfortunate reputation Filipinx have for being yes-people.

Spanish rule of the Philippines was constantly challenged by Indigenous rebels; the Moros—Filipinx Muslims—were particularly fierce and, for the most part, successfully resisted Christianization. My heart leapt when I read that perhaps the main reason the Philippine-American conflict careened into genocide was that, in the words of a US general, "practically the entire population has been hostile to us at heart."

José Rizal was a Filipinx polymath who lived his short but dynamic life in the second half of the nineteenth century. Conversant in twenty-two languages, he was every bit the "universal intellectual" so admired in the West, particularly Europe. He deployed these "white" attributes—especially his facility with language—to beat the colonizer at his own game. His books and essays, fiercely critical of Spanish authorities (the "double-edged Goliath" of corrupt friars and oppressive government), were widely credited for instigating Filipinx nationalism and, eventually, the Philippine Revolution of 1898. He was charged, arrested, and found guilty of sedition, illegal association, and inciting rebellion, and executed by firing squad in 1896, three years before the Filipinx genocide began in earnest.

(By devoting a paragraph to a lone, albeit brilliant, historical figure, the narrator is reproducing heroic liberal individualism.)

President Duterte. The product of centuries of Filipinx rage. Yes, he's a brute but he's the brute the West created. For Westerners, including Filipinx living in the West, to sit snugly and smugly back in their easy chairs and finger-wag about how horrible Duterte is, would be more amusing if it weren't such a nauseous display of hypocrisy. His immense popularity among the electorate is puzzling only to foreign observers who have no concept of how subjugated Filipinx have historically been. Duterte is simply the embodiment of a long-suppressed nationalist pride, and we all know what happens when something is suppressed for too long. When the white West cries foul at Duterte's human rights abuses, it is blind to the centuries of abuse the West has inflicted on Filipinx. I'm not a Duterte supporter, but I'm also Filipinx, and I feel the anger. The perverse rage of Duterte is the justified rage of an oppressed people.

I once confided in a good friend—a white man—that the fact that I knew so little about Filipinx culture, and was exposed to relatively little of it growing up, had finally caught up with me, in the form of extreme rage.

"At what?" my friend said. "It's up to you to educate yourself about your culture. No one else."

Again, I didn't challenge him; old habits die hard. But this friend—whom I've always known to be collectivist in his politics—was jettisoning society's responsibility to pluralism and placing the onus on the individual. Funny how humans, when feeling uncomfortable, will do one-eighties on even the most firmly held philosophical convictions.

———————————

Let's put rage aside for the moment; let's move on to joy.

I wasn't completely detached from my Filipinxness growing up. Not only did I speak Tagalog fluently until age ten, but Christmases provided me with overwhelming joy, mostly because of the Filipinx we surrounded ourselves with. I may not have cared much for most of them the rest of the year, but all that was duly forgotten every *Pasko*.

Christmas Eve is where it's at for most Filipinx. Music, both Western and Filipinx, pop tunes and Christmas tunes, I would play on the piano and everyone would sing along; food, food, food, something from and for everyone, *pansit palabok, pansit bihon, lumpia sariwa, lumpia shanghai, nilaga, caldareta, langonisa, kutsinta,* and rice, rice, rice, everywhere rice, endless overages of rice; the men smoking and drinking and playing cards in the kitchen, Mom and Lola chatting, gossiping and laughing with their wives, the other kids doing their thing and mercifully leaving me alone while I watched *The Sound of Music* on my own in the living room.

Then it was off to Midnight Mass—the only time Mom, Lola, and I ever went to church—at the cathedral on Main and 12th, whose congregation was at least eighty-five-percent Filipinx, one large, mostly brown, singing and worshipping and besotted organism. Didn't matter whether you bought into the lie that this was the Son of God's birthday—there were probably stragglers there who didn't believe in God at all—what mattered was what this communal connecting brought about: the weaving of an enormous thread, the temporary transcending of individual skin, the intangible surging warmth of a disinterested and pure love.

And on to beauty.

I'm currently obsessed with the paintings of Aaron Bautista. Born and based in Angono—popularly known as the Art Capital of the Philippines because of its rich artistic tradition—Bautista creates work that sings to me because of its liminality and in-betweenness, its gentle yet staunch refusal to be either wholly abstract or wholly representational, wholly urban or wholly pastoral, wholly Western or wholly Filipinx. He combines the ethereal all-over-ness of Jackson Pollock with the worldly specificity of Jean-Michel Basquiat. His liminality is effectively chimeric and therefore utopic.

(He is comfortable with Bautista's work because it reflects his own hybridity. Hybridity is self-undermining; hybridity is static. It elevates contemplation over action and is therefore inherently conservative.)

I've read that it takes at least two to three generations to overcome trauma, often more.

Systemic trauma is in my DNA. I can bleach my skin, refuse to speak Tagalog, but I cannot wish away my people's oppression. It's lodged inside me, manifesting itself in the anxiety, obsessiveness, paranoia, and feelings of worthlessness I confront every day.

For most of my life, I have tried to downplay or mask my Filipinxness. I realize now how I was perpetuating, on a personal level, my people's history of colonial erasure.

Although I accepted my queerness with relative ease, especially in comparison with many of my QTBIPOC friends, I wonder now if that ease was, at least in part, because of my desire to be white. Sexual nonconformity may be everywhere, but queerness is a white Western cultural construct.

It's all systemic. End of story. Or maybe I'm just crazy.

(It is *all systemic.* And *he's crazy.)*

October 17, 2015

Took me over 40 years, but finally hooked up with a flip.

N = muscular, early 20s bi stud. Fucked me lots. I came a lot.

Insecure though. Flexing in the mirror after he came, he started fishing for compliments. I gave him them but was sad about it, he should have no doubts about how gorgeous he is.

One-shot deal, this. That's okay. A quick fuck can be just as valuable as a 50-year marriage. And I'm grateful for the relative ease with which we queers understand that, and can dive immediately—without words—into the core of another person. As in right now, right away, without the rigamarole of all the "right things" you're supposed to say.

In an hour I got to his core—and to my own as well. And, I have to say this, something of the core of Filipinxness. I've heard some POC guys say that fucking a guy of the same race is narcissistic. I call bullshit on that—why don't they say the same thing about white-on-white sex? And is a little POC narcissism such a bad thing, given the white supremacy in the world?

Besides, the sex with N was unbelievable. Every joining and pressing an embrace of survival, an act of gratitude for being alive.

(He may have gotten over his white-only sexual leanings, but isn't he still an implicit body-shamer, going primarily for a particular, societally approved body type?)

The mirror.

Like most POCs, I've had a breakdown moment in front of the mirror, but not because I thought I was ugly. I'm not overly dark, my nose isn't flat, my lips aren't especially thick, and my eyes, though not heavily lidded like my mestiza Lola's, have enough of the European in them to dilute their ethnicness.

I broke down not because I thought I was ugly, but because I realized what yardstick I had relied on to reach that conclusion.

In that instant, it was as if the ground were pulled out from under me. Advancing, Platonically, from the physical to the spiritual, what implication did this realization have for the more intangible things in my life—to wit, the art that saved, edified, and advanced me, almost all of which was created by white Europeans and Americans? The boundless imagination of red-haired Anne Shirley; the exquisite coming-of-age of Lucy Honeychurch; the lyrical, existential despair of Blanche DuBois; the fastidious pathos of Gustav von Aschenbach; the infectious vibrancy of the men of Canal Street; the invigoratingly transformative thoughts of Sontag, Wittgenstein, Adorno, Foucault, Butler—what were the privileges that brought all this beauty to the world? And what were the processes that brought about these privileges? And on precisely whose backs were these privileges won?

Is the art I love, and will continue to love—and that has given me the only standards of creative excellence I really know, and has often been the only reason I've gotten up in the morning—all primarily something that emerged from the forehead of the colonizer? Is it all primarily the brainchild of the enemy?

Yes, I'm afraid. There's no escaping that fact.

So is the solution to be in the world but not of it? Is the world beyond repair, too fucked up to bother with? If that's the case, is individual liberation all we can strive for?

But individual liberation isn't entirely possible either, given how the idea of "liberation" is itself essentially colonial, conceptualized in the colonizer's language, inflected by middle-class heteronormativity and white supremacy. And to "liberate" as an individual means to play by the hegemon's rules, and be rewarded with "liberation" by the hegemon.

So we must engage with the world while aware of the divine, which will help us change the world as much as we can.

It starts with *language*.

In this book I've aimed for a high hubristic style, informed by the British and American essayists I've long admired. The arduous sculpting of each sentence to meet colonial standards—it's masochistic but meaningful work. I'd do it again. It's all I know.

But perhaps it's time I wholly embraced a different language, one fragmented and unapologetically biased, interrupted with silences that teeter on the abyss, that holds space for these silences and the new words that come out of them, a language that allows for the chronic perpetual potential of erasure by tenderly, triumphantly containing it.

Above all, though, I still crave beauty.

(The narrator's flip-flopping—pun intended—is making me crave a Dramamine.)

In the words of José Rizal: "When there is in nature no fixed condition, how much less must there be in the life of a people, beings endowed with mobility and movement!"

9 | CAESURA

VOICE PROPER (VP): I need to find my voice.

PARENTHETICAL VOICE (PV): *Your* voice. Neoliberal heroic individualism again.

VP: I admire you—most of what you say is correct and true. But the purity for which you advocate is not something I can ever embody. Your standards are as lofty as the Western high-art ideals that colonized me.

PV: And I'm colonizing you too, if nothing else than to get you to some reasonable place.

VP: But I can get nowhere at all, because I can barely move. I want to move sideways, and I want to move up, but there's gravity on all sides.

PV: What you're feeling is inertia. The inertia of self-hate.

VP: Probably. But I need the freedom to *not* hate that hate, to embrace it and use it to *move up.*

PV: Move up where?

VP: No clue. Just up. Or out. Beyond me. Beyond the confines of my brown skin. Beyond the confines of my queerness. Because there is an "out there" that all artists know intuitively. And our work needs to touch it if it's going to be anything but useless matter.

PV: And so you regard your brown skin and queerness as confining? Why not see them as instruments to freedom?

VP: I want to. I do. But I need to be able to envision what freedom looks like *for me.*

PV: Do you need to hate yourself to do that?

VP: Partly. And love myself narcissistically and love myself healthily. And love and not love others, and empathize and criticize. The only path to heaven is replete with thorns.

PV: So what's the problem?

VP: I didn't think you'd approve.

PV. I don't, I don't at all. But you don't need my approval. Do what you want, find your voice. Meanwhile, the city's burning. We'll get better folks to take care of that.

CADENZA, OR CODA

Dear Reader, the white spaces in this epilogue are for you.

Just recently I became aware that I am always clenching my fists

The staircase—still the place I feel most at home.

What queer Filipinx thinkers

I'm not going to be hypocritical, I'm going to be honestly critical about it. Tennessee Williams.

Ay, kuting-goy, kuting-goy! Kuting na, ungoy pa.

The forlorn beauty of unceded Coast Salish Territories in late October.

The coherence I see in the mirror

The ideal state is to be at home everywhere or nowhere. Susan Sontag.

The staircase remains bejewelled, but there are many different types of jewels now: emeralds, rubies, sapphires, as well as diamonds.

I'm doing it. I'm really doing it. Nathan, *Queer as Folk*.

Case-by-case approach

Yet despite being staged in seemingly bleak circumstances, queer of colour imaginaries are composed of utopic acts. Robert Diaz.

I have not mentioned my long-term relationship and continuing friendship with a beautiful, sensitive alcoholic. Another book.

Mental illness = a disease of Western civilization

Because you don't just hang out in a staircase, you need to actually do something there—either go up it or down. It has a clear intent and purpose and, at the same time, is not obtrusive.

The exquisite, extroverted Bombay cat I co-parent with my beautiful, sensitive, alcoholic ex.

Iyan, iyang ina mo, pinagsabihan na naman ako.

Where what counts is not the ideas or concepts of something

If I'm going to sing like someone else, then I don't need to sing at all. Billie Holiday.

And the fragmentation I'm told is my reality.

The old Filipinx folk tale of the selfish, rageful boy whose grandmother turns him into a monkey.

Loneliness festers that which is original, daringly and bewilderingly beautiful, poetic. But loneliness also fosters that which is perverse, incongruous, absurd, forbidden. Thomas Mann.

The divine means different things to different people. Two examples: 1. A puritanical utopia that stresses purity and sameness. 2. A pluralistic utopia that accepts and works with difference.

I will no longer beat myself up for enjoying
The novel is everything. Gertrude Stein.
Studying Guo Pei while listening to Callas

But the thing itself. What we need is less totalizing
Overreaching

On October 21, 2018, the *New York Times* reported the Trump administration's plans to legally define transgender Americans out of existence.

And since forever, being innocuous is what I've been.

Beethoven's *Appassionata* captures *striving*

And this time I'm for real
When I speak of this rebellion
And the urge I feel
I'm not sorry, not sorry
No, I'm not sorry, not sorry
No, I'm not sorry, not sorry
No, I'm not sorry, not sorry,
No
—Kimmortal

Sontag wouldn't approve of how personal this book is.

The violence you do to yourself when you see yourself only as an object.

Double melancholy = to live simultaneously in both *this* realm and *that*, to never feel at home in either, and to embrace this as the necessary condition.

On January 29, 2017, six worshippers were murdered at the Islamic Cultural Centre in Quebec City.

Poetry is not a turning loose of emotion, but an escape from emotion; it is not the expression of personality, but an escape from personality. But, of course, only those who have personality and emotions know what it means to want to escape from these things. T.S. Eliot.

The weird, disjointed, impure, uncoordinated, contradictory thing I see in the mirror is exactly as it should be, but *this* world tells me otherwise.

And more subtlety, texture, nuance from all sides. This is the only approach that can heal the divide plaguing all of us.

> *Sa isang madilim gubat na mapanglaw*
> *dawag na matinik ay walang pagitan,*
> *halos naghihirap ang kay Pebong silang*
> *dumalaw sa loob na lubhang masukal.*
> —Francisco Balagtas

Life is easy to chronicle, but bewildering to practice. E.M. Forster.

Cut down on the name dropping

I am mindful of my fists

The *madilim gubat* resists Apollo's garish forms, takes the light it wants but grounds deep in this *mapanglaw*.

My name is Christopher Edwin Gatchalian. I am a second-generation queer Filipinx settler born, nurtured, and based on the unceded ancestral lands of the Musqueam, Squamish, and Tsleil-Waututh peoples. I was raised primarily by my mother and grandmother, first in Richmond, then the West End, then finally East Van, where I lived until just a few years ago and which I still consider my cultural home. I am not certain of my ethnic makeup—"Filipinx" is a very general identifier, as it encompasses innumerable ancestries; what I *am* fairly sure of are my Chinese and especially Spanish ancestries, as these were the ones my family talked up. I wear masks well—people who know me will describe me as gentle and unassuming. In reality, I struggle with deep insecurities, fiercely, sometimes violently protective of myself and the space I take up in the world. I resort to passive-aggression, have been a bad friend, a selfish lover, and am a neglectful son. I will do better.

REFERENCES

Callas, Maria. *The Complete Studio Recordings (1949–1969)*. EMI Classics 0946 3 95918 2 4, 2007, compact discs, box set, compilation.

Davies, Russell, Sarah Harding, Menhaj Huda, and Charles McDougall. *Queer as Folk: The Complete Collection*. Silver Spring, MD: Red Production, 2011.

Forster, E.M. *A Room with a View*. New York: Signet, 2009.

hooks, bell. *Feminism Is for Everybody: Passionate Politics*. London: Pluto Press, 2000.

Mann, Thomas. *Death in Venice and Other Stories*. New York: Bantam Books, 1988.

Montgomery, L.M. *Anne of Green Gables*. Toronto: Tundra Books, 2014.

Paglia, Camille. *Sex, Art and American Culture: Essays*. New York: Vintage, 1992.

———. *Sexual Personae: Art and Decadence From Nefertiti to Emily Dickinson*. New York: Vintage, 1991.

———. *Vamps & Tramps: New Essays*. New York: Vintage, 1994.

Sontag, Susan. *Against Interpretation and Other Essays*. London: Picador, 2001.

———. *Illness as Metaphor and AIDS and Its Metaphors*. New York: St Martin's Press, 2005.

West, Cornel. *Race Matters*. Boston: Beacon Press, 1993.

williams, angel Kyodo. *Being Black: Zen and the Art of Living with Fearlessness and Grace*. New York: Viking Compass, 2000.

Williams, Tennessee. *A Streetcar Named Desire*. New York: New Directions, 1980.

Photo: Raymond Shum

C.E. GATCHALIAN is a queer Filipinx Canadian author and theatre-maker born, raised, and based on unceded Coast Salish territories (Vancouver). A graduate of the University of British Columbia's Creative Writing Program, he is a two-time finalist for the Lambda Literary Award, whose plays have been produced locally, nationally, and internationally. In 2013, he received the Dayne Ogilvie Prize, awarded annually by the Writers' Trust of Canada to an outstanding emerging LGBTQ writer. *Double Melancholy* is his first non-fiction book.

cegatchalian.com